THE COLLECTED PLAYS OF

THOMAS ALEXANDER

BOOK 1

Collected Plays: Book 1 by Thomas Alexander

Direct Light Publications
45 Dudley Court, Endell Street, London, WC2H 9RF

Copyright © 2014 Thomas Alexander. All rights reserved.

No part of this publication may be reproduced, transmitted, or performed in any form or by any means, electronic or mechanical, including photocopy, recording, or any information storage and retrieval system, without permission in writing from the publisher.

Permissions may be sought directly from Publishing Rights Department 45 Dudley Court, Endell Street, London, WC2H 9RF
Library of Congress Cataloguing in Publication Data
Application submitted.
British Library Cataloguing in Publication Data
Application submitted.
03 04 05 06 07 08 10 9 8 7 6 5 4 3
–

The characters and events in this book are fictitious. Any similarity to real persons, living or dead, is coincidental and unintended by the author.

Begat © 2010 Thomas Alexander
Great © 2010 Thomas Alexander
The Visitor © 2008 Thomas Alexander
All rights reserved.

Edited by Shirin Laghai for Direct Light Publications.

Cover Design by SimplyA

Thomas Alexander

FOREWORD

Two of the three plays presented here were written during a summer sojourn in Melbourne, Australia, in 2012. GREAT, the last of the plays to be written, was created in response to the attitude I saw against the UK while living in Australia, as well as the devolution and referendums on Scotland that dominated the years, post and previous. I used a line from The Waterboys song 'Old England' as a dedication in the original print, but in truth, though obviously I've known the song for decades, I didn't make the connection until about a year later.

I love London. Perhaps I'm not so enamoured with a lot of the other parts of the UK which, as William Gibson noted, has become the playground of oligarchs, but London is one of those truly great world cities that everyone should experience. It is a mess. It is broken. It is entirely beautiful and perhaps the last bastion to that American adage: 'Bring me your tired and weary.'

Still, living as I often do overseas, it is difficult not to see that England's - Great Britain's - day is over. It is an anachronism that hangs on by its fingers and all the cries of UKIP and The Sun or their opposites in The Guardian make not a hoot of difference. England is a dying animal, raging against the light. And, as in the play, we'd sell our souls for an iPad and a good wireless connection.

Begat came about from similar discussions. The rise of religious radicalism means that we are now living in a world of competing justice systems. From honour killings to denying passports to indigenous populations, we are at a cross-cultural turning point, and if two or more competing justice systems coincide then both will be considered unjust by the other. It is Israel and Palestine. It is the curse of globalisation.

The third play, The Visitor, dates much further back. It was started in novel form in Tokyo in 1997, and has been tinkered with ever since. It is, perhaps, the fundamental argument of my youth - love versus religion - and it takes a young man to try to attempt such a thing. Original drafts gave the Poet and the Priest no names and had no backstory whatsoever outside the final scene. But even at that stage of my writing I knew that this was too didactic, too preachy, for want of a better term, so I shelved it.

Strangely, as I've noted before, the focus of the play changed for me with the passing years. I no longer see the relationship between the Priest, Sarah, and the Poet as the central one. For me, the relationship between the Jailor and the Protégé - originally intended as motivation for the Priest's final actions – has come to the fore, and I think it is the truer and more enlightening of the three relationships presented in the play.

It has not gone unnoticed that all three plays have political overtones, though that was not the intent of this collection. They are, quite simply, the first three to go to print but, as with all writers, serendipity is something we are happy to claim as brilliance.

Thomas Alexander - 2014

ABOUT THE AUTHOR

Thomas Alexander has worked in almost all forms of theatre, from opera to children's performances, working as everything from stage hand to costume designer, and has seen his work translated into four different languages and performed as far afield as America and Afghanistan.

His complete plays, along with his first novel, *A Scattering Of Orphans*, have been published by Direct Light Publications.

Also by the Author

PLAYS

Happiness
Murder Me Gently
The Family
Begat
The Crossroads Country
Great
God
The Visitor
When Dusk Brings Glory
The Recruitment Officer
Writer's Block
The Last Christmas
Writing William
The Big Match

ONE ACT PLAYS

Four Widows and A Funeral
For Arts Sake
The TV
Life TM
The Dance
The Pink Cow

ADAPTATIONS

William Shakespeare's R3
Othello

NOVELS

A Scattering Of Orphans

CONTENTS

FOREWORD   page iii

THE VISITOR   page 1

BEGAT   page 87

GREAT   page 153

Thomas Alexander

THE VISITOR

THE VISITOR

CAST

NOTE: The central cast's ages have been left purposefully vague. There was a sense to the writer that the characters were people in their forties and early fifties but there is no reason to listen to him on this.

THE POET (PETER) Handsome, well dressed.

THE MISSIONARY (SANDY)

SARAH Attractive and well-dressed but not stylish.

THE JAILOR Sixties plus. Soft faced. Slim.

THE PROTÉGÉ Late teens to mid twenties.

PAUL Twenties. Suited. American.

GUARD Non speaking part.

VARIOUS VOICES ON TV

Thomas Alexander

ACT 1

SCENE 1

CURTAINS ON THE OUBLIETTE, A ROUGH PRISON HOLED FROM THE FACE OF A CLIFF, HIGH ABOVE THE COLD LATE AUTUMN LAND BELOW.

THE CELL, CARVED FROM ROCK, HAS A SINGLE DOOR – UPSTAGE – WITH A PEEP-HOLE NEAR THE TOP.

THE ROOM SEEMS TO BE EMPTY. WIND WHISTLES AROUND ITS CRAGGED SPACE GIVING IT AN UNWELCOME AIR. STAGE RIGHT, UNDER A BLANKET - THE SAME SHADE AS THE ROCK FACE - LIES THE PRIEST. HIS BRUISED AND BEATEN BODY, DIRTIED FROM THE OUBLIETTE'S DUST, MAKES HIM INDISTINGUISHABLE FROM THE WALL HE LIES AGAINST, FETAL AGAINST THE COLD.

ABOVE THE SOUND OF THE WIND WE HEAR THE SOUND OF AN OLD CHAIN LIFT, RATCHETING ITS WAY UPWARDS TOWARDS US.

REACHING ITS DESTINATION, IT STOPS AND WE HEAR THE SOUND OF A WROUGHT IRON GATE OPENING.

A PAIR OF FOOTSTEPS – ONE SURE OF ITSELF, THE OTHER NOT – WALK TOWARDS US. THE PEEP-HOLE SLIDES OPEN, REVEALING THE JAILOR'S FACE. KEYS JANGLE AND THE DOOR OPENS.

THE JAILOR OPENS THE DOOR, A CRACK AT FIRST,

The Visitor

AND THEN WIDE. HE STEPS ASIDE LETTING THE POET ENTER, WATCHING HIM CLOSELY AS HE DOES.

THE POET, STRONG AND HANDSOME, ENTERS, UNSURE OF WHAT HE'S LOOKING AT.

FROM HIS PERSPECTIVE THIS IS A CLIFF TOP, A CAVE, NOT A PRISON CELL. HE'S ABOUT TO TURN AND TALK TO THE JAILOR WHEN THE OLDER MAN SHUTS THE DOOR, AND LOCKS IT.

POET   Hey!

THERE IS NO RESPONSE. HE STARTS BANGING ON THE DOOR, AGAIN AND AGAIN, GETTING LOUDER.

POET   Hey! Hey, what is this? Hey!

THE PEEP-HOLE SIDES OPEN, REVEALING THE JAILOR.

POET   What is this? Let me out!

JAILOR   Two days. Then you go. Inspection. Yes?

THE PEEP-HOLE SIDES SHUT.

POET   Hey! HEY!

THE PEEP-HOLE OPENS AGAIN.

JAILOR   Two days. No more!

POET   What is this! Let me out!

THE JAILOR LOOKS AT HIM FOR A MOMENT, THEN SLIDES THE PEEP-HOLE SHUT AGAIN AND OPENS THE DOOR.

JAILOR   You want to go. Go. But deal's deal. There's no change.

POET   What is this? Alessandro Menine. You understand me? You don't get anything until I've seen

Alessandro Menine!

AT THE SOUND OF HIS NAME THE MISSIONARY MOVES, REVEALING HIMSELF TO THE AUDIENCE. HIS RIGHT EYE IS SWOLLEN SHUT, HIS FACE DIRTY, HIS SKIN MARKED WITH BRUISES.

JAILOR   So see him then!

THE JAILOR GOES ACROSS AND PULLS OFF THE BLANKET. THE PRIEST COWERS BUT THE JAILOR DOES NO MORE, AND RETURNS TO THE DOOR AND THE STARTLED POET.

JAILOR   Two days. No more.

THE JAILOR EXITS, LOCKING THE DOOR BEHIND HIM. WE HEAR THE SOUND OF HIS FOOTSTEPS LEAVING, THE GATE CLOSING, AND THE LIFT DESCENDING ONCE MORE.

THE POET STANDS THERE, STARTLED AT THE SIGHT OF THE MAN, SHOCKED BY WHAT HE'S SEEING AROUND HIM. HE TURNS IN DISBELIEF TO THE DOOR AGAIN.

POET   Hey! What the hell is this?

BUT THE FOOTSTEPS DON'T STOP. THE MISSIONARY, IGNORING THE PRESENCE OF THE POET, PULLS HIMSELF AGAINST THE WALL, GATHERING HIS STRENGTH. HE CROSSES, IGNORING THE POET AS HE HEADS FOR A FOOD CACHE STORED BEHIND A LOOSE ROCK IN THE FISSURE OF THE WALL, BEFORE MOVING BACK TO HIS POSITION UNDER THE BLANKET.

POET   (CONT.) Sandy? Alessandro? My god! Sandy. Sandy! It's me. Sandy? It's Peter. Peter Armitage?

The Visitor

You remember? Peter? Sandy? Sandy! Where is she, Sandy? Where is she? Sandy. Where is Sarah, Sandy? Where is she? Sandy! There's no record of her. I've asked everywhere. Did they take her? Sandy? Do they have Sarah? Sandy? Please, Sandy. I promise you! I can help you. I can help her! I just need you to tell me! Sandy? (HE DIGS SOME CHOCOLATE OUT OF HIS BAG) Jesus. Look at you. Sandy? Look. I can help you. Look. I have food. Real food! I think... I can get you out of here Sandy. I can! I can help you. Look, take it. Take it. I can help you, but I need to know. Do they have her? Sandy? Sarah? Do they have her? Is she still in the country? Is she? Sandy? (THE MISSIONARY LOOKS AT THE PROFFERED CHOCOLATE) Yes. Take it. Take it! Really. I can help. I can. Is... Is she still in the country? Sandy? I can help her! (THE MISSIONARY STANDS AGAIN, PUSHING ANGRILY PAST THE POET) Damn it, Sandy! Let me help you!

MISSIONARY Get away from me!

POET   Sandy!

MISSIONARY Get away from me!

POET   Sandy. Listen to me. I can help! Just tell me! Tell me! I've... I got access to the prison records. All of them. She's not on any of them. Did they take her, Sandy? Is she still in the country?

MISSIONARY (QUIETLY) I reject you.

POET   What? Sandy? Sarah, Sandy. Do they have her?

MISSIONARY (LOUDER) I reject you!

POET   Sandy? Jesus, man, It's me, Peter. Sandy? I can help her, Sandy. I promise I can. I just have to know. Sandy? Do they have her? Is she safe?

Thomas Alexander

THE MISSIONARY TURNS AND WITH VIOLENT STRENGTH THROWS THE POET TO THE GROUND, BEATING HIM WEAKLY WITH HIS FISTS.

MISSIONARY I reject you! I reject you! You're not real, do you hear me! You're not real!

POET Jesus, Sandy! What the f… It's me! Peter!

MISSIONARY I will not have you here! Understand me! I will not have you here! I will kill you! I will…

THE POET GAINS CONTROL OF THE WEAKENED MAN AND RESTRAINS HIM. THE MISSIONARY STARTS TO CRY.

POET Get off me! Stop it! Stop it, Sandy! Stop it! I don't want to hurt you but I will if I have to, so just stop. Alright?

MISSIONARY You're not real.

POET I am, really. I am. I… I promise.

MISSIONARY I don't want you here.

POET I am real. I promise you. Look. (HE PLACES THE MAN'S HANDS TO HIS FACE) I am real. Feel me. Feel me. I'm real. I'm really here. I promise. It's me. Peter.

THE MISSIONARY BREAKS DOWN, TEARS FALLING DOWN HIS FACE AS HE HUGS THE MAN IN FRONT OF HIM. THE POET, UNCERTAIN AT FIRST, HUGS BACK.

POET I'm really here. I promise.

END OF SCENE 1.

The Visitor

SCENE 2

LIGHTS UP ON THE DOWNSTAGE AREA. A HOTEL ROOM. LIGHTS FADE ON THE OUBLIETTE

SARAH ENTERS, THROWING HER COAT ONTO THE BED. SHE IS SOAKED TO THE SKIN.

SARAH   I can't believe you're really here. (SHE TURNS AND LOOKS BACK AT THE DOOR, SMILING) Don't be silly. You can come in. Really. I'm not going to bite.

ENTER THE POET, LIKEWISE SOAKED.

POET   You're sure. I mean…

SARAH   I promise. You (BEAT) might find a few inappropriate garments strewn around - I really haven't had time to clean – but I've removed all the bear traps, promise.

POET   Ha. No it's just, you know. I didn't know if you're… I don't want people to get the wrong impression.

SARAH   Yeah? And what impression would that be? Wet?

POET   You know what I mean.

SARAH   (MOTIONING TO A CHAIR) Put your coat there. You want a towel?

POET   Please.

SARAH   We're old friends. Let them get whatever impression they get. Jesus. I'm soaked through. Here. (SHE TOSSES HIM A TOWEL) I'm going to change.

EXIT SARAH.

SHE EXITS BUT CONTINUES TALKING OFF-STAGE. THE POET MOVES AROUND THE ROOM LOOKING AT VARIOUS PERSONAL EFFECTS.

SARAH   (CONT., OFF) I'd offer you a change of clothes or something but somehow I don't think you'd fit in my dress.

POET   Oh, I don't know.

SARAH   (OFF) I heard that! Anyway, all I've got is summer stuff. So unless you want to go strapless…

POET   Could be a bold new beginning!

SARAH   (OFF) The transvestite poet? You'd go down a hit in Lower Kensington.

POET   I'm already a hit in Lower Kensington. Upper, too!

SARAH   (OFF) What will the drawing rooms of Knightsbridge do with you? You want one of these robes?

POET   Towel's fine.

SARAH   (OFF) Can you believe it? I didn't even bring an umbrella.

POET   That's the problem with these summer countries. You think it's all going to be one heat wave, and suddenly it's Noah's ark out there.

ENTER SARAH.

CHANGED INTO A SUMMER DRESS, THE BACK IS STILL OPEN.

SARAH   Think we should have grabbed some animals on the way in? I saw a couple of rats in the foyer. Here, get this for me, would you?

POET   (ZIPPING HER DRESS) There're a couple of cockroaches under the bed, but I think they may be hermaphrodites. So we may only need one. Fancy playing god?

SARAH   (TURNING AND IGNORING THE JIBE)

The Visitor

So how long you been here anyway? Please, sit anywhere. You want a drink?

POET   Um. Sure. Coffee?

SARAH   No, I mean a drink!

POET   (SMILING) Oh, I see. Well in that case… Definitely.

SARAH   (FIXING A DRINK) How long you say you've been here?

POET   A week. I've got to tell you. I'm a little… What's the word.

SARAH   Discombobulated?

POET   (TAKING THE DRINK) Thanks. Discombobulated. Exactly.

SARAH   I know what you mean. I saw you in the foyer… This morning? You were coming out of the elevator as I was going in. To breakfast, I suppose. You didn't see me. Or did you?

POET   No, I had no idea.

SARAH   So I've had, like, a few more hours than you to get used to it. But discombobulating. Definitely. Can I do that? Verb the word?

POET   I have absolutely no idea.

SARAH   And there's you, the author.

POET   Poet. Actually.

SARAH   Didn't you write that… thing?

POET   Maker's Mark?

SARAH   (SMILING) I didn't want to…

POET   Remember the title?

SARAH   Inflate your ego.

Thomas Alexander

POET   It's about how you see yourself. Novelists are… I don't know.

SARAH   Unromantic?

POET   Well paid. No. It's just… It helps you keep things straight, you know what I mean? I'm a poet. A poet who happens to also write a novel or two. It helps keep things in perspective.

SARAH   In that case, can I still do this? May all of your rhymes, fit in their lines, and if they don't, just say fuck it. Cheers.

POET   (LAUGHING) Jesus. Cheers. You know, not every poem in the world has to start with: there was a young man from Nantucket! There is such a thing as free verse.

SARAH   And free towels as well. (MOTIONING FOR THE TOWEL) Give that here. (MOTIONING TO THE DRINK) You want another one?

POET   (FINISHING IT QUICKLY) Sure.

SARAH GOES OVER AND STARTS POURING ANOTHER DRINK.

SARAH   God. I tell you. I really can't believe you're here.

POET   You know, I'm sorry but… I didn't think you could do that.

SARAH   Drink?

POET   Swear.

SARAH   Was I swearing?

POET   God? Taking the Lord's name in vain.

SARAH   Yeah. Bad habit. I probably got that from you. (SHE HANDS HIM HIS DRINK) So what are you doing here? Writing?

The Visitor

POET   Lecturing. One of the universities is giving me an honorary degree. You know how it is. They're translating some of my collections into the local language and I'm giving a series of lectures at the campus. It's all embarrassing really.

SARAH   No, it's not!

POET   It is. Really.

SARAH   "The poor man's Ted Hughes."

POET   (LAUGHING) Oh, god. You don't want to take any notice of that! I think my publisher came up with that one.

SARAH   No, I'm proud of you. We all are. We always were.

POET   Well thank you, but really. You don't want to believe everything you read in the press.

SARAH   And you met the queen?

POET   I did. That I did. Meet the queen.

SARAH   She's something, isn't she?

POET   You met the queen?

SARAH   We were doing one of the charity things. You know how it is.

POET   Yeah. And that's what you're doing here now?

SARAH   I am, actually. Yes. You didn't see the posters?

POET   Sorry.

SARAH   Downstairs? In the foyer? We're having a fund-raiser. Tonight. You know I work with the CPA now, right?

POET   I'm sorry, I…

SARAH   Well, I've been working with them for the past few years. Arranging funding, you know, for the schools and - well pretty much everything, really. You've no idea how much it costs.

POET   To run a church?

SARAH   Is that what you think I do? Run a church?

POET   Well, I mean. The missionary's wife…

SARAH   There's… We started this school. An orphanage originally, after the outbreak, but it's pretty much everything now. Boarding school, adult learning centre. And you wouldn't think these things cost a lot of money. You know, not there. I mean it's just wood and books, right? But well, first there's the bribes… Talk about charity! For every pound we want to spend on, you know, important things, we have to spend another two bribing people to let us build it, or stop them from tearing it down. Really. It drives me indiscriminately nuts! I'm not kidding.

POET   People have a very narrow view of who is their own.

SARAH   So, anyway. It costs, all of it. So I work on the money. The CPA do good work, don't spend it all on administration, if you know what I mean. So I help them set up fund-raisers. Things like that. Turns out I'm pretty good at it. Talking people out of their money.

POET   I have no doubt that you are.

PAUSE.

THEY ARE BOTH ASHAMED AT THE GROWING CHEMISTRY BETWEEN THEM.

SARAH   What was it? OBE?

POET   MBE. It's nothing.

SARAH   No. I tell you, if it makes it onto the BBC World Service, it's not nothing!

The Visitor

POET   Is that where you heard it?

SARAH   I was cooking.

POET   You used to burn water!

SARAH   I wasn't that bad.

POET   You remember that time, at your parents' place. You insisted on cooking for Jeremy and me, and you made that fried pork?

SARAH   Oh god!

POET   Crispy on the outside, bloody in the middle.

SARAH   Jeremy was sick for a week. He never forgave me.

POET   How is your brother?

SARAH   Good. Good. You know. Something in the city, or whatever they call it these days.

POET   And your husband?

SARAH   Sandy.

POET   Right.

SARAH   He's good. Listen. I'm, you know… There's no easy way to say this. I'm sorry… For not inviting you to the wedding…

POET   No, really.

SARAH   It was just…

POET   No, I understand completely.

SARAH   It would have been…

POET   We were kids.

SARAH   We were.

POET   And anyway, I was out of the country.

SARAH   Well, there we are then.

POET	I couldn't have come anyway.
SARAH	Where were you?
POET	Paris.
SARAH	Really?
POET	What?
SARAH	We… You were really in Paris?
POET	Why not?
SARAH	Paris? Not, you know, Paris Texas or something?
POET	What's so…
SARAH	We were married in Paris.
POET	Really?
SARAH	In really Paris. I kid you not.
POET	Huh.
SARAH	You didn't know that?
POET	You never sent me an invite.
SARAH	Point. And you're not…
POET	No. Never.
SARAH	Wow.
POET	What?
SARAH	Well. You say that so absolutely.
POET	Do I?
SARAH	You do.
POET	Yeah, well. (BEAT) He doesn't mind? You travelling so much?
SARAH	He does. Of course he does. But it's for the school, and well….
POET	(SHIVERING) Jesus. You know the other

The Visitor

problems with places like this?

SARAH　　　　Air conditioning?

POET　　　　You know, I swear to god if they'd invented air-conditioning two hundred years earlier the entire world would be run by the Chinese. The only reason England did so well was that we didn't need siestas. (MOTIONING TO LEAVE) I should…

SARAH　　　　Listen. Come tonight. Are you free?

POET　　　　To the charity thing?

SARAH　　　　Yes, come! Are you free? You should come. Really. You'd love it. Well. Okay, that's not true. I usually hate the things, but it'll be a big crowd thing and…

POET　　　　I'm supposed to meet some professors…

SARAH　　　　Blow it off. Or better yet, bring them! Seriously. You'll be a huge hit. Which, in turn, will make me a big hit. Which, in turn, will allow me to relieve them of all their hard earned cash!

POET　　　　I don't know.

SARAH　　　　Please. Come. I don't see many people from, you know, home. And it's too big a coincidence, us running into each other here.

POET　　　　Serendipity.

SARAH　　　　Divine intervention. I just don't want it to be a five minute thing, you know what I mean? I bump into you. You bump into me. We both get soaked in a rainstorm, and then I never see you again.

POET　　　　How long are you in town? I've got some things I can cancel tomorrow…

SARAH　　　　I'm flying back in the morning.

POET　　　　(BEAT) Then, of course. I'll come.

Downstairs?

SARAH   Downstairs. In… (SHE JUMPS UP) God. An hour. I've got to…

POET   You look great. Don't worry.

SARAH   Yeah, right.

POET   I'd better make some calls.

SARAH   Alright.

POET   You want me to come back here or meet you downstairs?

SARAH   Here. We'll go together. What room are you in?

POET   Four-o-two.

SARAH   I'll come to you.

POET   See you in a bit, then. Do you want me to, you know… Read something? I don't know…

SARAH   Just come.

POET   Thank you.

HE MOVES TO EXIT AND THEN TURNS AGAIN.

POET   Sarah. Listen. Not for nothing, but… You look… Fantastic. I just wanted to…

HE EXITS. SARAH WATCHES THE DOOR, THEN SITS, THE SMILE FADING FROM HER FACE.

END OF SCENE 2.

The Visitor

SCENE 3

LIGHTS DOWN ON THE HOTEL ROOM.

LIGHTS UP ON THE OUBLIETTE.

THE POET AND THE MISSIONARY SIT ACROSS FROM EACH OTHER, LOST IN THOUGHT. THE MISSIONARY IS EATING THE CHOCOLATE.

POET	How long have they kept you like this?

MISSIONARY I'm... I haven't spoken to anyone in a long time. I'm not used to it.

POET	(STANDING) What is this place?

MISSIONARY It's an oubliette. A cave. They were... Prisoners... You can jump. It's your choice. You can stay here or you can jump. I think they're waiting for me to...

POET	Why haven't you?

MISSIONARY (JOKING) Suicide's a sin.

POET	How the hell did you get yourself into this?

MISSIONARY What's happening? Outside?

POET	There's... I don't know. I don't really watch the news anymore. They finished the election, finally.

MISSIONARY The country. What's happening with the country?

POET	I'm... You know as much as I do. The border's still closed. They're not talking to the outside world. The rest is... anyone's guess, I suppose. I didn't see anyone else. On the way up. I didn't see anyone else. No corridors. No rooms.

MISSIONARY At the top of the butte. There's a prison at the top. Twenty or so, I think.

POET	I didn't even know they had buttes.

Thomas Alexander

MISSIONARY Greek. Originally. Oubliettes.

POET Well, I like what you've done with the place. Airy.

MISSIONARY Bijou.

POET Very... monkish. Birdshit's a nice touch. Pre post-modern, if you know what I mean.

THE MISSIONARY BURSTS INTO A COUGHING FIT.

POET You must be important to keep you here alone.

MISSIONARY They think it's... poetic.

POET And they've kept you here all the time?

MISSIONARY City. Then they brought me here.

POET Alone?

MISSIONARY Alone.

THE MISSIONARY MOVES TO HIDE THE REST OF THE CHOCOLATE.

POET So that's the choice, is it? Stay here or jump? No, eat it. I have more.

MISSIONARY Storing. Some days... They stop. Or forget. I can't tell which. I... I thought you were a ghost. I thought... I thought perhaps I'd gone mad, you know. I kept thinking I would. I kept... I talked to things. At first. I sang. Birds come in here sometimes. Crows. Checking... I talked to them at first. It was... ironic. I think. I was a man worried about madness, but I thought maybe I was going mad. I was losing... So I stopped. I stopped talking to them. The birds. And I thought, perhaps you were because of that. I thought because I'd stopped talking...

POET Where is she?

The Visitor

MISSIONARY I thought, of all the things that I could create, of all the people... You... Do you understand?

POET Where is she?

MISSIONARY See, God... If this is all some kind of test. From God? Well, God I can handle. God has a purpose, but my mind... You understand.

POET Is she still in the country?

MISSIONARY What happened to Navratil?

POET They shot him.

MISSIONARY Really.

POET In the square. And in the head. In that order. Couldn't have happened to a nicer guy.

MISSIONARY You ever seen anyone shot?

POET No.

MISSIONARY Then you don't know what the hell you're talking about.

POET I... bribed. I bribed a lot of people. Revolution is a costly business it seems. There was this man, in the central bureau. That's what they're calling it now. Bureau au Politic. He got me a list of foreigners who were being held. Your name was on it. With this address. I don't know any more than that. You're costing me a fortune.

MISSIONARY You're not doing it for me.

POET No.

MISSIONARY When did...?

POET I see her?

MISSIONARY The last time.

POET (PAUSE) I heard from her about eight months ago. A phone call. She was fading in and out. It was already underway by then. She said you were getting out of the country. Both of you. I figured it was just a question of waiting. So I waited. Four months ago the CPA contacted me, asking if I'd heard from her. I got in touch with the consulate but... There was no record of you crossing the border. Not that that was terribly unusual. I spoke with your church...

MISSIONARY You spoke with the church?

POET For all the good it did me. Turn the other cheek seems to be the motto when dealing with warlords and dictators. Finally I spoke with a camera crew. American. They told me they'd helped you. Been working with you at the... Well, mission, they called it. Before the uprising.

MISSIONARY Did they mention anything about a boy? Kinhio?

POET I... I wouldn't have known to ask.

THIS HAS A GREAT EFFECT ON THE MISSIONARY.

POET (CONT.) The one thing I couldn't find any record of... was her.

MISSIONARY You can get me out of here?

POET Maybe. I think so. Not from here. I mean, these guys are as greedy as the next guy, but the jailors here aren't going to just let you out. No matter what the price. They'd be killed. The new regime... I can get you out. I know I can. But I need to be on the outside. Now we know where you are...

MISSIONARY You can smell things, sometimes. On the wind. You can smell... Cooking? They had a bag on my head when I came here. Is there a camp at the bottom?

POET There's a house. A guard's house, I guess. There's a chimney.

The Visitor

MISSIONARY I'd never thought of it.

POET What?

MISSIONARY Are they married, do you think? I never really thought about it before. Is there a wife at the bottom of the cliff, cooking supper for them?

POET I wouldn't know.

MISSIONARY It's… I've never thought of them outside the context of… this.

POET Why the hell were you doing to them? Proselytizing….

MISSIONARY (LAUGHING) Proselytizing , yes. That was it! It doesn't matter.

POET What did you mean before? Loved her.

MISSIONARY The boy? The one I mentioned before. He was with me when I was arrested. We were… We were driving back into the city. It's… We think fighting starts in the cities, don't we. Usually not. (BEAT) We never even made in back into the centre.

POET I can help you. I can. From the outside. But Sandy…. If she's in prison. If she's being held. Whatever you think of me. I can help her. I can. You just have to tell me. You just have to…

MISSIONARY (VENOMOUSLY) You use… You use emotions like words. Like I use words.

POET Does it matter? If she's safe, does any of it matter?

MISSIONARY It's sickening. How long were you lying with my wife?

THE POET LAUGHS.

MISSIONARY (CONT.) What?

POET   No. Lying? Lying? Is that what they teach you in… I'm sorry. It's just…

MISSIONARY   Six years? Give or take?

POET   None of that matters…

MISSIONARY   It matters! Of course it matters! It matters to me. You really expect me to help you? You?

POET   I expect you to help her! Whatever you thought of her, she was with you! She was your responsibility! Yours! Jesus, man. Let me help you! Let me help her. What…?

THE SOUND OF THE LIFT CHAIN ASCENDING STARTS. THE MISSIONARY RISES, MOVING TO THE EDGE.

MISSIONARY   They're coming.

POET   What do you…?

MISSIONARY   I… Leave me alone.

POET   Jesus. Move away from the edge!

MISSIONARY   Leave me alone!

POET   Don't be stupid. They're probably just going up!

THE LIFT CRANK STOPS AND WE HEAR THE DOOR SLIDE OPEN. THE MISSIONARY RETURNS TO HIS PLACE.

MISSIONARY   No no no no no no no.

POET   What..? Sandy? Sandy?

THE PEEP-HOLE SLIDES BACK AND THE PROTÉGÉ LOOKS IN. IT SLIDES SHUT AGAIN AND THE DOOR OPENS.

POET   Hey, can we get some help in here?

ENTER JAILOR AND PROTÉGÉ.

The Visitor

THE PROTÉGÉ IS ARMED.

JAILOR   (TO THE POET) Sit over there.

POET   What's…

THE PROTÉGÉ STEPS UP AND POINTS THE GUN DIRECTLY AT THE POET'S HEAD.

PROTÉGÉ   He said get over here!

POET   (MOVING AWAY) Jesus! Fine. Fine. Whatever. Just… Get that thing out of my face!

JAILOR   You get what you want?

POET   What? No! I…

PROTÉGÉ   Should maybe have talked faster.

JAILOR (TO PROTÉGÉ) Get his arms.

THE PAIR PULL AT THE ARMS OF THE SITTING MISSIONARY WHO WHIMPERS BUT DOESN'T RESIST.

POET   Where are you taking him?

JAILOR   You want to go?

POET   I have two days! You said two days!

PROTÉGÉ   Stay where you fucking are, man. I mean it!

THE PAIR BEGIN TO DRAG THE MISSIONARY OUT OF THE ROOM. THE POET STAYS ROOTED TO HIS CORNER.

POET   Sandy! Sandy! Where are you taking him? Sandy!

SUDDENLY HE JUMPS UP IN FRONT OF THEM.

POET   This is ridiculous!

PROTÉGÉ   Get the fuck back!

POET   (TO SANDY) Where is she! Tell me! For

god's sake!

MISSIONARY Dead.

THE PROTÉGÉ PUSHES THE POET BACK TO THE FLOOR AND THE THREE EXIT, DRAGGING THE MISSIONARY BETWEEN THEM. THE DOOR SLAMS SHUT LEAVING THE POET ALONE IN THE CELL.

END OF SCENE 3.

SCENE 4

LIGHTS UP ON THE BEDROOM. SARAH IS ALONE IN THE BED, SLEEPY. SHE WAKES, CHECKS THE CLOCK, THEN PULLS THE COVERS OVER HER HEAD AGAIN.

THE LIGHTS FADE ON THE OUBLIETTE.

ENTER POET.

HE COMES IN QUIETLY, THE LIGHTS HALF ON, AND SITS GENTLY ON THE SIDE OF THE BED WATCHING SARAH SLEEP.

SHE STIRS, SEES HIM THERE, TURNS AND SITS UP RUBBING HER EYES.

SARAH	You scared me.
POET	Sorry.
SARAH	I was asleep.
POET	Sorry.
SARAH	You just getting in?
POET	Yeah, I'm sorry. My… The flight was delayed.

THE VISITOR

I tried to use one of those phones they've got there, but I didn't know the hotel number and…

SARAH   I was asleep.

POET   Yeah. Come here.

THEY HUG.

SARAH   I must look terrible.

POET   Well…

SARAH   I was asleep!

POET   So you keep saying.

HE KISSES HER PASSIONATELY BUT SHE PULLS AWAY.

SARAH   I'm… Oh, god, what time is it?

POET   Four.

SARAH   I was dreaming. I… How did you get in here?

POET   Stanzas.

SARAH   I'm sorry?

POET   The girl at the front desk. I wrote four stanzas on the Dubai experience. (BEAT) I'm kidding. The room's in my name remember? Go back to sleep. I'll take the couch and…

SARAH   No, I'm up. I'm up. I'm… I'm sorry. It's… It's wonderful to see you again. It's just…

POET   I know. Don't worry about it.

SARAH   I'm not used to this.

POET   Me too. How's the charity?

SARAH   CPS?

POET   It's CPS now?

SARAH   Yeah. Ridiculous, isn't it. You know what the

problem is? Money. You want coffee? (HE SIGNALS NO) These things all start out with the best of intentions, you know, and they… (SHE YAWNS) They start out with the best of intentions and then they make money. And suddenly, you know, it's a full time job, so you've got to pay someone and it grows and suddenly there's logistics and it's too big for one person and before you know it half the money you're making is being spent on administration. And suddenly it's not a charity anymore, not really. It's an organization. You know? And you start to wonder, don't you? Is it really worth giving money to these people so they can keep driving… Whatever they're driving. It's ridiculous.

POET   I can't stand the fact that all men start out with the idea of Madonna and end with the reality of Sodom.

SARAH   That you?

POET   Dostoevsky. Basically.

SARAH   Big on pop singers, was he?

POET   What's the solution?

SARAH   I have no idea. The little charities. They do good, but they can't reach the places the big ones can so…

POET   You keep reinventing yourselves.

SARAH   If the governments…

POET   Oh, god. Politics at dawn. Very sexy!

SARAH   I know. I'm sorry. Not the kind of thing you really want to hear, is it.

POET   No, it's… fine. Really. This is part of who you are and… I want to hear about you.

SARAH   Not exactly Last Tango in Paris, is it?

POET   Oh, sweetheart! I've been on a plane for eighteen hours. You start a tango and it's going to aggravate

The Visitor

my deep vein thrombosis.

SARAH I was having the strangest of dreams.

POET Come here.

SARAH LAUGHS GIRLISHLY AND CRAWLS ACROSS THE BED TOWARDS HIM. THEY KISS, BECOMING PASSIONATE, AND FALL BENEATH THE COVERS.

THEY BREAK. SARAH SNUGGLES INTO HIM.

SARAH I missed you.

POET I always miss you.

SARAH (SUDDENLY AWAKE) What time's your thing in the morning?

POET I'm not even sure what morning it is!

SARAH I set the alarm for eight.

POET I'm still on LA time.

SARAH …'M fading.

POET I know.

SARAH Can you sleep?

POET As soon as my brain passes the Christmas Islands. Don't worry about it.

SARAH 'Kay. I really missed you.

POET Go to sleep.

HE SITS THERE FOR A MINUTE WATCHING HER, THEN UNTANGLES HIMSELF AND STANDS SLOWLY, MOVING AWAY FROM THE BED.

LIGHTS FADE ON THE BED.

END OF SCENE 4.

SCENE 5

LIGHTS UP ON THE OUBLIETTE.

THE POET IS ALONE IN THE ROOM, WAITING AND REMEMBERING, HIS MANNER ANXIOUS AND CONFUSED.

WE HEAR THE SOUND OF THE ELEVATOR, RATCHETING DOWN TOWARDS US.

THE POET RISES AND LOOKS AT THE DOOR. WE HEAR THE STEEL GATE PULLED BACK AND FOOTSTEPS COMING TOWARDS US.

THE POET PACES.

THE DOOR OPENS AND THE THREE RE-ENTER, DRAGGING A BARELY CONSCIOUS AND CLEARLY TORTURED MISSIONARY. THE JAILOR AND THE PROTÉGÉ KEEP THEIR EYES ON THE POET AS THEY DEPOSIT HIM ON THE OTHER SIDE OF THE OUBLIETTE.

JAILOR   (TO POET) Do you have anything to say? About your friend? Nothing?

POET   He's not my friend.

THE JAILOR NODS AND TURNS AWAY. THE PROTÉGÉ FINISHES DUMPING THE BODY.

JAILOR   (TO PROTÉGÉ) Come.

THE TWO MEN LEAVE. THE PROTÉGÉ MAKES A THREATENING GESTURE TO THE POET AND IS PLEASED WHEN HE FLINCHES.

THE POET WAITS UNTIL THE TWO MEN LEAVE AND THEN HURRIES OVER TO THE PRONE BODY,

The Visitor

SHOCKED AT WHAT HAPPENING BUT RESOLUTE.

POET   Jesus! Sandy? Sandy?

MISSIONARY Cold.

THE POET MOVES HIM, COVERING HIM WITH BOTH THE BLANKET AND HIS OWN COAT. HE SHIVERS IN THE WIND. THE MISSIONARY WATCHES HIM BLANKLY.

POET   Where is she? Sandy? Where is she! Do you hear me? Sandy? Damn it man, they're… You've got to tell me where she is! I can hel…

MISSIONARY I told you. She's dead.

THE POET SITS BACK.

POET   Bullshit.

MISSIONARY You don't believe me?

POET   If she was dead I'd know.

MISSIONARY Fire. They set her on fire. All of them. It wasn't personal. It was a matter of expediency, nothing more. Women burn white. You know that? Fat content. Men burn orange but women burn white.

POET   You're lying.

MISSIONARY Simpler than arresting them. Simpler than waiting them out. They simply burnt the building down.

POET   Stop it.

MISSIONARY They took them out of the church and shot her in the head.

POET   Before or after they burnt them alive?

MISSIONARY She contracted AIDS. A bad needle, nothing more.

POET   It's not funny.

Thomas Alexander

MISSIONARY (LIFTING HIS SHIRT PAINFULLY) Tomorrow I'll bleed painfully from places you never want to see blood come out, so why don't you let me be the judge of what's funny or not.

THE TWO ARE SILENT FOR A FEW MINUTES.

POET What the hell did you do to them?

MISSIONARY (LAUGHING) I did nothing to them! I did nothing to anybody!

POET You... Why did you bring her here? You knew it was dangerous! After Zambia? How could you have made her come here with you!

MISSIONARY I couldn't make her do anything, and she didn't come here for me.

POET Of course she came here for you. For your stupid religion...

MISSIONARY You don't know what you're talking about.

POET For your crusade! She came here because you told her to come.

MISSIONARY No.

POET She came here because you told her it was the worst place in the world, because you told her it was where she was needed the most!

MISSIONARY You're wrong.

POET She was a sucker for a bleeding heart and you told her to come here.

MISSIONARY She came here to escape you! (PAUSE) You know nothing about her. Nothing. You think saying something and meaning it is the same thing. It's not! You think you loved her. Is that it? You think... You are such a fool. You knew nothing about her. Nothing. (PAUSE) You... It was her idea

The Visitor

to come here. Did you know that? After Zambia? It was her idea! I wanted to take her home. I was offered a church. A... I wanted her to be near family. Friends. You, even. I... She chose to come here. She spoke to the deacons... She wanted to get away from you.

POET   You were working with the FRJ. Is that why?

MISSIONARY You don't know what you're talking about.

POET   The FR...

MISSIONARY What is that? Is that a name you read in the newspapers? Is that what that is? FRJ? There was no rebellion! There were no rebels! It's... It's got to be a story, doesn't it? The world. It has to fit into neat little narratives? This side or that. Is that it? Companies evil, governments good. Governments evil, rebels good. Is that what it is? It doesn't work like that. People are mean and stupid. People are mean and stupid and God loves them. That's all there is. There are no rebels. There are no struggling masses. People hurt people. There's no organization about it. There doesn't have to be. FRJ? I never met anyone from any group calling themselves FRJ, yet the world thinks that every teenager with a gun is that.

POET   The FRJ are the people who helped me get in here.

MISSIONARY No, they weren't. People pick up a name. They need a banner. FRJ, IRA, al Qaeda – they're as good as any. People pick up names.

POET   Which one was she working with?

MISSIONARY Let me sleep.

POET   What the hell is it with people and countries. I get... I can understand the idea of fighting for something you believe in. I can understand wanting to pick up arms and right an injustice. But a country? Land. Stupid antiquated notions that mean nothing. (BEAT) One person at a time.

MISSIONARY (PAUSE) When I came here, I don't know.... There were... They'd closed the churches. All of them. It didn't matter what denomination. It didn't matter what anyone believed. You believed in the country or you believed in nothing. You know what a country is? It's what you know. What you know! The food you eat. The way you talk. Sports. Language. That's all it is. A country. When I came here... When we came here. It was stupid, that's what it was. You hear, you hear about landmines aimed at children, you know, toys... And you hear about roadside bombs, indiscriminate. You hear about all this but you don't hear what living with this kind of life does to people. What it... People hate each other. There's no trust, and when there's no trust there's fear and anger and...

PAUSE.

POET   She told me you were coming here with the mission.

THE MISSIONARY NODS.

POET   (CONT.) She kept changing charities... I mean. It wasn't enough... (HE SMILES) She used to complain, did you know that? All the time. She used to complain about each of them. Each one. She'd join a new charity like they were the second coming and then six months later she'd be all over them. Hating them.

MISSIONARY I had to stop her giving away everything we had.

POET   Were you in the capital during the coup?

MISSIONARY Just outside it. We heard it though. Heard it all the way down the road. That's another thing that changes. In... We're used to hearing it on the TV, you know? I was in

The Visitor

London during the bombing. (PAUSE) We both were. First thing we did was turn on the TV. Turn on the TV to find out what's happening outside our door. Here it's rumour. It's whatever someone tells you. That's what you tell other people. And soon everyone believes the same thing. Or different things. And that becomes the truth. Boy robs a store – it's the FRJ. A family are killed in their home – it's the government. Doesn't matter if it's true. It's part of what it is.

POET What do they want from you?

MISSIONARY You think you know her, but you don't. You get to meet people. Good people, bad people. Same people you want to bring medicine in, bring guns. Same people. Humanitarianism and inhumanity go hand in hand. You want to get things done in… You've got to… Corrupt people are corrupt on all levels. Guns, secrets, medicine. It's all the same. You're shipping one, you're shipping them all. You know nothing about her.

WE HEAR THE SOUND OF THE ELEVATOR COMING UP. THE MISSIONARY WINCES AND PULLS THE COVERS OVER HIM.

POET People cause their own misery. Why get involved?

THE PEEP-HOLE SLIDES BACK.

POET (CONT.) For god's sake man, just tell them! If there's something you know, tell them! It can't do them any good now!

THE MISSIONARY IS SILENT.

THE POET GOES UP TO THE DOOR, ANXIOUS AGAIN. THE PEEP-HOLE SLIDES OPEN AND THE PROTÉGÉ LOOKS IN.

POET This wasn't part of the deal!

Thomas Alexander

PROTÉGÉ   Step back.

POET   He's no good…

PROTÉGÉ   Step back!

THE POET STEPS BACK AND THE DOOR OPENS.

THE PROTÉGÉ ENTERS CARRYING A TRAY WITH TWO BOWLS OF GRUEL.

PROTÉGÉ   Room service!

POET   This wasn't part of the deal. He's no good to me dead! Two days!

THE PROTÉGÉ IGNORES HIM AND MOVES ACROSS TO THE MISSIONARY, WHO STAYS PRONE ON THE FLOOR.

THE PROTÉGÉ KICKS HIM.

PROTÉGÉ   Still with us, Father? Yeah, you're still here, aren't you, shithead. Soup time!

POET   He needs medical attention!

PROTÉGÉ   Yeah? Need medical help, do you Father? (HE KICKS HIM AGAIN) Want me to take you back upstairs? Put a little band aid on it for you, Father?

POET   Stop it. He's not Catholic!

PROTÉGÉ   See, he doesn't need a hospital, do you Father? No. See. He's fine! Isn't that right, Father?

POET   I get two days. That's the deal!

PROTÉGÉ   (GIVING HIM THE BOWL OF GRUEL) You get what I give you. Ain't that right, Father? Yeah. You get what I give.

POET   There's to be no more torture! Not while I'm here. Tell your boss that!

THE PROTÉGÉ TURNS, HIS DEMEANOUR

The Visitor

CHANGING.

PROTÉGÉ   Listen. You a writer then, are you?

POET   Why?

PROTÉGÉ   How do you get into that, then? You need schooling?

POET   I don't know. Not really.

PROTÉGÉ   What kind of thing you write?

POET   I'm… I'm a poet. Mainly. A couple of novels.

PROTÉGÉ   TV?

POET   No. That's… It's a different medium.

PROTÉGÉ   Yeah. (BEAT) You like my English?

POET   I don't…

PROTÉGÉ   I learnt it off TV. Good yeah? How'd you get into writing TV?

POET   I… I wouldn't know.

PROTÉGÉ   Not much of a writer then, are you? Two days. Room and board. Nothing more. And we do to him what we like. Be thankful we don't do to you.

HE TURNS TO GO AND THEN TURNS BACK.

PROTÉGÉ   (CONT.) Forgot to bless the soup.

HE SPITS INTO THE POET'S BOWL, TURNS, AND AS AN AFTERTHOUGHT KICKS OVER THE BOWL.

PROTÉGÉ   (CONT.) See you tomorrow, Father!

THE PROTÉGÉ EXITS.

WE HEAR THE SOUND OF FOOTSTEPS, THE DOOR, AND THE ELEVATOR DESCENDING. THE MISSIONARY TRIES TO GATHER THE LAST OF THE BROTH ON THE FLOOR.

POET What on earth can it matter? Now. For god's sake, just tell them what they want to know. Everyone's probably either dead or gone anyway.

MISSIONARY (LOOKING UP) Now, yes. I told them everything on the first day. In the first ten minutes.

END OF SCENE 5.

SCENE 6

LIGHTS DOWN ON THE OUBLIETTE. LIGHTS UP ON THE BEDROOM.

SARAH IS SITTING ON THE BED, AN ANGER SUBSIDING IN HER.

THERE IS A KNOCKING AT THE DOOR. SARAH IGNORES IT.

A PAUSE, THEN THE KNOCKING INCREASES.

POET (OFF) Sarah! Open the door!

SHE CONTINUES TO IGNORE IT, THE ANGER GROWING ONCE MORE. SHE PULLS A SUITCASE FROM UNDER THE BED AND BEGINS TO PACK.

POET (CONT., OFF) Sarah! Dammit! Stop being such a child! The room's in my name, for Christ's sake. You want me to go back down to the desk and get another key?

SHE STALKS ACROSS AND OPENS THE DOOR, BEFORE RETURNING TO THE BED ONCE MORE.

POET You're leaving? Great. That's just great. One fucking fight and you leave me. Him…

The Visitor

SARAH   Oh, grow up! It's not… This is stupid. I don't want to have this argument!

POET   So much so that you'll throw us in rather than deal with what's really going on here!

SARAH   What's…? Oh, that's rich! What's going on is I'm leaving.

POET   (CLOSING THE BAG ON HER ANGRILY) No, you're not. You're staying here and we're going to deal with it! It's been three days, Sarah. Three days! Three days and you decide you can't live with me? It usually takes women the better part of six months to learn they can't live with me!

SARAH   Is that supposed to be funny?

POET   I didn't…

SARAH   Great. Six months. I'm a fast learner. This was a mistake. Is that what you want to hear? This is a mistake!

POET   Sarah…

SARAH   And I'm not just talking about this. All of this. It was a mistake. I don't know what I was thinking. Jesus. I must have been crazy.

POET   Can you just… Just stop. For a minute. I'll call you a cab if you like. I'll do it myself. There's not going to be any flights at this time anyway but… Please stop. For a minute.

SARAH   I wanted romance. Just a little romance, you know? I'm… That's all I wanted, alright? Just romance. To feel… All this… I'm married. Married. You understand that? Married! And I love my husband. Really. He is twice the man you are. On his worst day he is twice the man you are! This… I wanted a bit of romance. That's all! To feel…

wanted! I should never have… It didn't mean anything, you understand? It…

POET　　　　　Stop. Just… Stop. I didn't hear anything after married.

SARAH　　　　Why did you… What made you think…

POET　　　　　Just…

SARAH　　　　It was a sin. I knew it. A sin.

POET　　　　　Oh, bullshit!

SARAH　　　　It was. A sin! A sin against God. Against my husband…

POET　　　　　Bullshit! Bullshit! You want to… You want to pretend this was just… something? Go ahead! You want to make like it didn't mean anything to you, fine. But don't bring your bullshit religion into it! This has nothing to do with God. Nothing!

SARAH　　　　It was a sin! You can't even understand that. I was, Jesus, I am, cheating. It doesn't matter what you believe. It's a sin!

POET　　　　　You think this is good for me? You think this is easy?

SARAH　　　　Fucking another man's wife? Yeah, it's really hard!

POET　　　　　(VIOLENTLY ANGRY) Do not..! Do not call it that. I've fucked. I've fucked a lot of times…

SARAH　　　　I'm sure you have.

POET　　　　　This was not fucking. It wasn't! If there was ever a definition of making love it's what we have. Leave your fucking God out of it! You want to leave, leave, but do not – do not – belittle what's between us.

SARAH　　　　You can't stand it, can you? People with

The Visitor

faith? All your talk of beauty and existentialism but you can't even extend that far, can you.

POET   I have no problem with people believing...

SARAH   You can't stand it! There is a God! I believe that! There is a God and he watches and judges...

POET   Jesus.

SARAH   And he judges. Me! He judges me! When I'm with you, he judges me!

POET   Do you even listen to yourself?

SARAH   You will never understand our faith.

POET   Our faith?

SARAH   Yes. Our faith! What, did you think I didn't believe as well? Did you think I was just a missionary's heathen wife?

POET   I believe. I have faith! I have faith in people and...

SARAH   Jesus!

POET   I have faith in people and ideas and community...

SARAH   Words! All of it. You have faith in words! You talk and talk but it's all just words. What do you do? Nothing? You do nothing! You write words and you think that makes you an expert? On people? On faith? You think that makes you an expert on what anyone but you thinks?

POET   You know what I think? I think you can't walk away so you're burning it all down. That's what I think. (SILENCE) I think you saw something tonight that frightened you. Something that...

SARAH   (SOFTER) What am I doing here, Peter? What…. This dress? Those people…

Thomas Alexander

POET   It was an award dinner...

SARAH   And that's your life, isn't it. What did you call it?

POET   (JOKING) Epicurean?

SARAH   Those people. Those terrible, terrible people. I...

POET   They're just people. You deal with people like that all the time! The charity...

SARAH   I'm on the other side from them. I... They're... I don't talk to them, not like that. I don't. We talk about the charity. I didn't... What purpose did I have? What reason? What reason did you have? I was watching you up there on the podium and I just kept thinking how stupid it all was. All of it! How pointless. And you, with your words, with all those beautiful words, how pointless you seemed to me. How stupidly pointless.

POET   I'm sorry to hear that.

SARAH   And there it is! First time tonight. I've finally hurt you, haven't I?

POET   Have you ever stopped to think? Have you ever... An area is starving. People are dying. You go in there with medicine and food and keep them alive. You keep them... They're dependent on you! They're dependent! The area couldn't support that many people in the first place and you just gave them a life, a life to have kids, which you'll also keep alive. And now there're too many people in the region and they're dependant on you. Totally dependent. All the irrigation in the world isn't going to keep that many people alive in an area like that, and no one likes being dependent, so they... They grow up. They grow up and fight. Each other. You. They breed and kill and hate because that's the only thing they can, other than wait for you to put more rice on their table. You don't move them to another area which can support them. You can't! The people living there won't let you, and you can't bring them back to civilization. There's too many of them!

SARAH   You don't know what you're talking about.

POET   Don't I? Have you ever stopped to think…

SARAH   Fuck you. Civilization? Fuck yourself!

POET   Alright…

SARAH   You help the ones in front of you. You help the ones that need help. It isn't about them. You can't even see that! It's about you. You!

POET   That's just a little selfish, isn't it.

SARAH   Selfish is thinking that just because other people might cause more problems for you, you should let them die.

POET   Alright. I didn't mean that.

SARAH   It won't work. Can't you see that?

POET   You're talking about us?

SARAH   We're different worlds. Completely different.

POET   I know this. Walking out now… Walking out won't make it work. I… I love you. I know you think that's easy for me to say and everything, but it's not. You go home every time to him and it hurts. But I stay alive because I know, in reality, you love me too. I know… Tonight was a mistake. I'm sorry. It was a mistake. You've given him eight years. Give me one week. That's all I'm asking.

SARAH   We have, anyway.

POET   What?

SARAH   Six months. You said it took women six months to know they couldn't live with you. We met again six months ago. Tomorrow.

POET   It was just a stupid line.

SARAH   Isn't that what they always are? Lines? Goodbye Peter.

EXIT SARAH.

FADE TO BLACK.

END OF SCENE 6.

SCENE 7

LIGHTS DOWN ON THE BEDROOM.

IT'S SUNSET IN THE OUBLIETTE. THE LAST VESTIGES OF THE SUN ARE FALLING OUT OF THE ROOM, SHROUDING IT IN DARKNESS.

THE MISSIONARY IS SITTING IN HIS CUSTOMARY POSITION RESTING AND WATCHING THE POET AS HE WRITES SOMETHING ON A PIECE OF PAPER GLEANED FROM HIS BAG.

MISSIONARY It's beautiful, isn't it?

THE POET LOOKS UP.

MISSIONARY (CONT.) Horror from beauty.

POET   (LOOKING OUT TO THE HORIZON) Is that Kardisn? To the left over there?

MISSIONARY When does it happen, do you think? At some point… People move from wanting to be left alone, to… One

The Visitor

minute you're a family, thinking about work and… dinner and… and grandchildren, and the next you're a mob, walking down the street, intent on killing some group of people you don't even know. How do they go back to it, do you wonder? Doesn't it seem… false. (PAUSE) What are you writing?

POET　　　　Something. I'm not sure yet.

MISSIONARY There's this thing… A myth. The Lords of Shouting. Beautiful, really. They… Every morning ten million angels sing to God as he pushes the sun up into the sky. Beautiful. And I've often wondered… What happens at sunset?

POET　　　　That's Jewish, isn't it?

MISSIONARY Kabbalah, I think.

POET　　　　I didn't think you'd care about Jewish mysticism.

MISSIONARY Comparative religion. Second year of university. (PAUSE) Can I read it?

POET　　　　Perhaps. When it's finished. The light's gone now. It's too dark. (PAUSE) Anyway, it is sunrise, right?

MISSIONARY What do you mean?

POET　　　　Somewhere. If the sun's going down here, somewhere…

MISSIONARY I'd never thought of it like that.

POET　　　　It means the Lords must always be shouting.

MISSIONARY Maybe there're different ones. For each country.

POET　　　　Maybe it's only over Zion.

MISSIONARY Somehow I doubt that.

THE SUNLIGHT HAS ALL FADED.

Thomas Alexander

A SMALL PATCH OF MOONLIGHT ILLUMINATES THE FRONT OF THE OUBLIETTE, DIPPING OVER THE CLIFF INTO THE CAVE BEYOND. THE MAJORITY IS, HOWEVER, COMPLETELY BLACK.

MISSIONARY She was eighteen when I met her. Did she tell you that? You didn't come to the wedding. She'd mentioned you, of course. I'd never heard of you. Even when you became famous, I didn't hear of you. Except from her.

POET   I know all this.

MISSIONARY We met at a seminar on Matthew – the gospel. The Kingdom of Heaven I think it was. She was only eighteen, but bright... You know her father was a preacher, I suppose. One of those lay preachers. The kind that stand behind a wooden pulpit and bark out the fear of damnation. Why weren't you at the wedding?

THE POET LIGHTS A CIGARETTE IN HIS CORNER OF THE OUBLIETTE, IT LIGHTING HIM FOR A MOMENT.

POET   I was out of the country. Cigarette?

MISSIONARY I don't smoke.

THE POET LAUGHS AND THROWS THE PACKET WITHIN REACH OF THE MISSIONARY. A LIGHTER FOLLOWS. THERE'S SILENCE AS THE MISSIONARY LIGHTS ONE AND COUGHS AT HIS FIRST SMOKE.

POET   I met her first when I was, what was it, eight? Ten? I don't remember. My friend was in love with her. We had a house in her town and we used to spend the summer there. He was a local boy. Kept telling me about her. I saw her through a window in the back of her father's car. Nothing more than that. She never mentioned you. At the college.

MISSIONARY She used to argue with the lecturers. Always

THE VISITOR

arguing. The Eucharist, Augustine... I don't think there was anything she didn't disagree with.

POET   It was her father's idea. University. She told me she'd made a pact with him. A degree in theology and he'd let her go her own way. It was her way of being...
Such a useless thing. Religion.

MISSIONARY Like poetry.

POET   Poetry doesn't start wars.

MISSIONARY Then what's the importance of it? (PAUSE) How do you do that, anyway?

POET   What?

MISSIONARY Become a poet.

POET   How do you become a missionary?

MISSIONARY Is there a job application or something? Or do you just decide you're going to do it? How... Who buys poetry? Seriously. How on earth can you make a living writing poetry?

POET   A strong knowledge of verbs.

MISSIONARY And yet your... How many houses do you have? It must be nice coming from privilege.

POET   Yeah, listen. I'm not about to compare what we do or anything, but I work hard for what I get. I spend six months of the year travelling...

MISSIONARY Listen to yourself! You go around the world collecting platitudes from people who don't know any better. And for what? What was that last one?

POET   Euripides. It was a collection about Euripides.

MISSIONARY (LAUGHING) Well, that's just classic isn't it. Yes. Way to give back something to the world with that one.

POET It's not like you're employable in any other part of the world, is it? I mean, missionary? Really? In this day and age? Have you ever noticed that people who work in churches are the kind of people who could only get a job writing articles for a local newspaper? Wanted, saving the world through Jesus. Must be articulate, irrational, and able to obstinately adhere to a set of doctrines that would make Pol Pot look like a humanitarian. What on earth makes you think there's a God?

THE POET'S CIGARETTE DIES DOWN AND HE STUBS IT OUT.

MISSIONARY Not in here. Throw it over the cliff. If you throw it in here they'll notice.

THE POET STANDS AND MAKES HIS WAY TO THE MOONLIT EDGE.

POET I just don't understand how someone with… Someone who's seen as much as you have can believe in God? The Christian God. How do you reconcile it? How do you… keep believing?

HE TOSSES THE BUTT OVER THE EDGE OF THE CLIFF.

POET (CONT.) Jesus, it's cold. If winter…

THE MISSIONARY COMES AT HIM OUT OF THE DARK, DRIVING HIM TOWARDS THE EDGE, HOPING TO THROW HIM OVER. THE TWO MEN HIT THE FLOOR INCHES FROM THE EDGE, THE MISSIONARY ON TOP.

MISSIONARY (SCREAMING) I am your God! I am your God! You have worshipped at my table! You have worshipped at my table!

The Visitor

THE POET THROWS THE WEAKENED MAN OFF AND THE TWO STARE AT EACH OTHER ACROSS THE MOONLIGHT.

POET   Get off me! Get off me! What are you, crazy? You could have killed us both!

MISSIONARY She was my wife!

POET   You could have killed us!

MISSIONARY She was my wife! My wife!

HE BEGINS TO CRY.

THE MISSIONARY HAS BEEN SCRATCHED IN THE FIGHT AND HE CHECKS HIMSELF FOR BLOOD, HOLDING HIS HAND UP TO THE MOONLIGHT.

POET   Jesus! (PURPOSEFULLY) Jesus! You could have killed us both!

MISSIONARY (LAUGHING) I should stay alive so my wife's lover can come by for visits? Should I expect poems? Cigarettes? This is supposed to mean something to me?

POET   I'm the only thing keeping you alive and you know it!

MISSIONARY (CRAWLING BACK INTO THE DARK) What makes you think I want to live? Get out of here. Just... Get out.

POET   Where is she buried?

MISSIONARY No.

POET   She's alive, isn't she?

MISSIONARY No more stories. Go.

POET   I'm not leaving until you tell me.

SILENCE.

MISSIONARY Pray there's a God. Pray to him. I swear. Pray

to him they kill me because I promise, I will kill you. If you stay here I will kill you. Pray for that!

POET   How did she die?

FADE TO BLACK.

END OF ACT I.

THE VISITOR

ACT II

SCENE 1

LIGHTS UP ON THE BEDROOM.

THE POET IS SITTING IN THE BED, HIS OWN, WATCHING A DRAMA ON TV. A REMOTE IS IN HIS HAND, A BOOK IN THE OTHER.

M1 TV   …I don't care.

M2 TV   We all have our roles to play, George. Just because you've stepped down doesn't mean the game doesn't go on. You know that. Someone has to keep the wolf from the gates.

M1 TV   I'd say it does.

M2 TV   Don't be a foo….

HE IDLY CHANGES CHANNELS, FLICKING FORWARD TO A NEWS PROGRAM. IT SUCCEEDS IN GAINING HIS ATTENTION.

NEWS TV   …where reports of continued unrest have been coming in. The earthquake, measuring 7.8 on the Richter scale, has been seen by some as the final nail in the coffin for the Korinov government. Government aid workers have continued to lobby for support but…

THERE'S A RING ON THE DOORBELL. HE SILENCES THE TV AND CHECKS HIS WATCH. THE DOORBELL RINGS AGAIN, INSISTENTLY.

HE RISES AND GOES TO THE DOOR, UNCONCERNED ABOUT HIS STATE OF DRESS.

ENTER SARAH, BREEZING PAST HIM INTO THE ROOM.

SARAH　　　　Did you see it?

POET　　　　I'm watching it now. I didn't think you were getting in til tomorrow.

SARAH　　　　I've been here for a few days. He's flying out tomorrow.

POET　　　　(PROCESSING) Okay.

SARAH　　　　You answer the door like that?

POET　　　　I wasn't expecting anyone.

SARAH　　　　(LOOKING AT THE MUTED TV) The stupid… If they'd just let the international agencies in…

POET　　　　Apparently they're beginning to open up.

SARAH　　　　Not fast enough. No government agencies. Only charities. Who the hell do they think funds the charities in the first place?

POET　　　　Strangely, I thought I did. You didn't tell me you were getting in earlier.

SARAH　　　　(AS THOUGH SEEING HIM FOR THE FIRST TIME) Hey. Yeah, I'm sorry. I… I hate lying. You know that. I thought it would be better for you…

POET　　　　Don't worry about it. Come here.

SHE SMILES AND MOVES INTO HIM, KISSING HIM PASSIONATELY.

SARAH　　　　You smell of hotel bedsheets.

POET　　　　Would you like to?

SARAH　　　　(LAUGHING) Get off! I haven't… I need a shower.

POET　　　　(HEADING OFF STAGE) What do you think they'll do?

EXIT POET.

The Visitor

SARAH STANDS WATCHING THE TV. PRESENTLY WE HEAR THE SOUND OF A SHOWER RUNNING.

SARAH Let their people die. 7.8 and they all live in concrete bunkers. The death toll… I read the book.

ENTER POET.

POET What was that?

SARAH I read the book.

POET Come in the shower with me.

SARAH Did you hear what I said?

POET I heard. Come in the shower with me.

SARAH Don't you want to know if I liked it?

POET Are you saying you didn't?

SARAH A little obvious, don't you think?

POET The themes?

SARAH (SERIOUS) The inscription. It's…

POET I thought you'd like it.

SARAH I… I do, but… He's not stupid.

POET He's never going to read it.

SARAH And the people I work with? The people you work with? They're not stupid either. We've been out together. I've been your other at award ceremonies. People…

POET I don't care. I'm sorry. Yes. You're right. People aren't stupid. Let them make of it what they will. But please, don't ask me to care.

SARAH You can be so naïve, sometimes.

POET I wrote worlds for you and the only thing you have to say about it is the inscription?

SARAH You wouldn't understand.

POET	Maybe I understand too well.
SARAH	Silly bear. (PAUSE) I'm going.
POET	(CONFUSED) I just ran the shower…
SARAH	(POINTING TO THE TV) No, there. I'm going there. We just got clearance.
POET	We.
SARAH	It's part of the mission. They're giving clearance to the religious organizations and…
POET	When.
SARAH	Tomorrow. We fly to Turkey and then…
POET	This is what you came here for, is it? To tell me?
SARAH	I wanted to see you.
POET	To tell me you were going there? Great!
SARAH	Don't be so melodramatic!
POET	What if there's another earthquake? That's not out of the realm of possibility! And the government? What if there's a coup?
SARAH	We're linked to the UN…
POET	What if they decide you're better to them as a western hostage? It's not like it's the first time they've tried that trick.
SARAH	It's where the people are!
POET	It's too dangerous! He must be out of his mind!
SARAH	They need help!
POET	Let him go! Let him preach hell-fire and damnation to a people who just saw it with their very eyes. Like that's going to go down well.

The Visitor

SARAH   That's not what…

POET   Stay here. With me. Let him go. You've done enough. Haven't you done enough? I don't think I can stand another Zambia. Another Zambia.

SARAH   It won't be like that.

POET   How in the name of hell would you know? Seriously. You can't promise me that! You can't! This… This is one of the most closed countries in the world, for god's sake. They don't have dissidents, they have martyrs.

SARAH   That has nothing to do…

POET   I can't. Seriously. I… I didn't know. In Zambia. No one told me! Do you understand that? No one told me. It was… I was at a party, for god's sake. I was at a party and this woman… This stupid woman started telling it like it was an anecdote. Weeks, weeks later. I had to sit there. I had to sit and listen as this stupid woman… Do you know what that did to me? Do you know? I couldn't reach…

SARAH   Hush.

POET   I can't go through that again. I…

SARAH   Hush now.

POET   I nearly jumped on a plane. Then and there. It was all I could…

SARAH   I have to go. Don't you see that? You think it would be any different for him…

POET   I don't care…

SARAH   But I do. I… I love you. And the book…

THE POET GETS UP AND STARTS TO MOVE UPSTAGE, TOWARDS THE OUBLIETTE.

POET   Stay.

SARAH	You help the people in front of you.
POET	I'm in front of you.
SARAH	It's not the same thing. You don't need my help.

HE MOVES INTO THE OUBLIETTE. HEADING TO HIS USUAL SPOT.

POET	I do. Really. I need it. I need you.
SARAH	You can't have me.
POET	Why? Why is that? Why can't I have you?
SARAH	Because I'm dead, silly.

END OF SCENE 1.

SCENE 2

LIGHTS DOWN ON THE BEDROOM. LIGHTS UP ON THE OUBLIETTE.

THE POET IS WAKING, RECOVERING FROM HIS DREAM. A FEW FEET AWAY THE JAILOR IS STUDYING HIM CAREFULLY.

THE MISSIONARY IS ABSENT.

JAILOR	Good. You're awake.
POET	(LOOKING AROUND) Where is he?
JAILOR	I thought perhaps we would chat a little. In private.
POET	Where have you taken him?
JAILOR	He is quite safe. I have been asking around

The Visitor

about you. You understand? It is not often a man buys himself into a jail cell. Out, yes. But not in.

POET   I have one more day.

JAILOR   He is a friend of yours? (SILENCE) No, I didn't think so. You do not act like a friend. My, how is it, my protégé, is that the right word?

POET   It'll do.

JAILOR   My protégé. He thinks he has treasure hidden. He thinks you buy your way in here to ask him about this treasure. He is young. He watches too many movies. (THE POET IS SILENT) I have been asking around about you. At the border, yes? They tell me you crossed without passport three weeks ago. They tell me you came illegally. Is this true?

POET   Does it matter?

JAILOR   To me? No. You want to crawl yourself into this hell hole, then fine. You have money, you can have service! This is the way of the world. Yes? You come to us and you say, let me in to see prisoner. Half now, half later. That is fine. This is the way. But I am thinking. I am thinking. How do we know you have more money. You come across border. This is great risk. You cannot bribe border guards. Ours, yes. Easy. But the other side? And yet, no passport when they search you. I think you do not want to be known.

TOO LATE THE POET NOTICES THAT HIS BAG HAS BEEN MOVED. THE JAILOR HAS BEEN THROUGH IT.

JAILOR   (CONT.) So, question I ask myself. How you know he is here. Answer is money. Of course. But you know where! You know who to ask. This is exceptional. You are not soldier, you are not spy!

Thomas Alexander

POET   Is that right?

JAILOR   No. You are not spy. No craft. No... You come here. Loud. Money everywhere. This is good. This is the right way, but you do not hide it. Or cannot. No, no spy. That is not important. Besides, we have him three months. You know? There is no secret in him.

POET   And yet you continue to torture him.

JAILOR   Which you mind? Yes?

POET   If he knows nothing...

JAILOR You have money. You are smart. But you are risk. Great risk. Coming in here. This is special prison. Geneva Convention? This does not fly. Outside world knows they create problems, I think. Perhaps for me?

POET   The outside world doesn't care about anything you do. No oil.

JAILOR   Indeed. No oil! Still risk. Maybe when you leave I take money and kill you? I don't. But is risk nonetheless. Yes?

POET   Spit it out.

JAILOR   Boy, he watches TV. Me, I read. I read you. Long time ago. I almost forget. I lived in New York. Cab driver. You believe that? Five years! Long time ago. New life. My daughter there. But I miss the old country. You understand that? No. I don't think you do. You have no country, do you? No country, no money, treasure. No secrets. So I think to myself, what is there? No money, no country, no secrets. Someone? Yes? Someone. (HE PULLS A BOOK FROM THE POET'S BAG) Her, someone? (SILENCE) You are romantic. You are hero. You love someone very much, I think. Not family. Not like this man. Not religion. I thought religion, but no. Not religion. Not god religion anyway. Woman. Woman, yes? His

THE VISITOR

woman?

POET   What did you think of the meter? I was never happy with the meter?

JAILOR   You know nothing of what happens here. You know nothing of what happens to this man. You worship, yes, but not god. Woman! What kind of fool is that?

POET   The kind that doesn't torture other people.

JAILOR   That right? You think so? What you think? You don't torture this man? Loving his woman? You know nothing of what happens here. Nothing!

POET   Enlighten me.

JAILOR   What means this, please? En…

POET   Tell me.

JAILOR   You maybe write poem about me, yes?

POET   If you like.

JAILOR   If you like. I had woman. Wife. Daughter. I was government, you believe this? Long time ago. Then came the war. You know this? The war? I was government so they take my wife. My son. My daughter, she is at school, safe, but they take my wife. Kill her, yes? Easy. This is war, killing is easy. They take my son. Don't kill him. Take him. What are they thinking? What? Maybe they think war will go bad for them and better to, ah, blackmail, this is right? Blackmail?

POET   I'm sorry to hear that.

JAILOR   But, they win war. Ha! I am exile. I run. Like rabbit. Like father. I run. New York. New life. But my son. My son, he is here. Somewhere, I think. I think. He is maybe alive. He is not, but I think it. So I return. It is five years, yes? Government changed, once, twice, three… Bad place.

Thomas Alexander

We are... Too much history. Too many memories. Sides. My grandfather town attack your grandfather town. Let's war! I search for him. I find records. This, we are good at! Records! I think you find that, yes? A remainder of communism. He is alive for two years. Two years. What they do with him in this time? I don't know. He is six. Why keep him alive? Then he is dead. Bullet. Gone. And I am here. This is our story. This is our history. You understand?

POET   I understand.

JAILOR   No. I think you don't. To you we are... amoral. That is your word. (HE TAPS THE BOOK) Here. Amoral! No Genève code. No goodness. We are backward country the world tries to forget!

POET   This man. The man you are imprisoning. The man you torture. He cared. When the earthquake...

JAILOR   Ah, the earthquake! Yes. Drama! To you, this is drama. This is shame. Poor people. Now they must open their borders! Now they must welcome the world. Forty years until communism. Did you come then? For that earthquake? Did you come for the camps? For our fathers? Tell me, what can you do more about? God's hand on earth or man's hand on our necks? I do not judge you. I live in America too. (PAUSE) You go now.

POET   I'm not ready.

JAILOR   If he does not tell you where she is now, he is not likely to.

POET   I have one more day!

JAILOR   (PREPARING TO LEAVE) Suit yourself (HE RAPS ON THE DOOR) Find her soon, is my advice. Today we try new torture. I do not think he lives after that.

FOOTSTEPS ARE HEARD COMING TOWARDS HIM.

The Visitor

POET Why? Why? He knows nothing. Nothing you don't already?

THE JAILOR LOOKS AT HIM AS IF THE QUESTION IS STRANGE.

JAILOR The boy must learn. (THEN AS IF TO CLARIFY) Protégé? The boy must learn!

THE DOOR OPENS AND THE PROTÉGÉ PUSHES THE MISSIONARY INTO THE CELL AHEAD OF HIM, HIS HANDS BOUND. HE FALLS HARD TO THE FLOOR.

JAILOR Two hours. Two hours then we start. (BEAT) Before lunch.

THE PROTÉGÉ GIGGLES AND THE PAIR LEAVE THE ROOM.

THE MISSIONARY LETS OUT A HOWL OF DESPERATION.

POET Stop! Sandy. Stop. Look at me. What the hell's…

MISSIONARY Leave me alone.

POET Stop it!

MISSIONARY This…

POET Sandy!

MISSIONARY No! This is what they do to religion…

POET Listen!

MISSIONARY They bleed it! They burn it! Beat it out of you!

POET Sandy!

MISSIONARY The great atheist! The humanitarian.

POET What the hell are you talking about?

Thomas Alexander

MISSIONARY Two hours…

POET I… They're cleaning the cell. That's all. Stop it. They're cleaning the cell! God, I don't know, someone's coming I suppose. That's why I can't stay here after tomorrow. There're important people coming. They're reviewing your case!

MISSIONARY Get away from me!

POET They're reviewing your case. They were just telling me. I think they'll let you go.

PAUSE.

SILENCE.

POET (CONT.) Sandy…

MISSIONARY You're a good friend, Peter. You're a good friend. You were a good friend to her. I know that. Here. After Zambia. You were a good friend.

POET We… I never… We weren't trying to hurt you.

MISSIONARY You're a good friend. A good friend.

POET I'm… She loved you. It's…

MISSIONARY Yes.

POET That was never in doubt.

MISSIONARY No.

POET I was…

MISSIONARY You're a good friend.

POET She was never going to leave you.

MISSIONARY (SIGH) This is what they do to men of faith. This is what they do! We believe so they break us. They beat us. This is what they do. You're the humanist. How can you not believe in truth that has to be beaten out of you?

The Visitor

SILENCE.

POET　　　　I suppose… What made you decide? You know, to believe? What made you… I mean…

MISSIONARY My Damascus moment?

POET　　　　Yes.

MISSIONARY I was… I was young. Youth. You believe anything when you're young. You believe people in power, your teachers, your betters… You think they must be better than you. Smarter. You believe anything when you're young. Is that hope, do you think? That what youth is? Hope. (BEAT) I was baptised at fifteen. I went to seminary… Now, when I think about what I believe, why I believe… Faith is the belief in something other than yourself. Something you can't truly know. Something… bigger. I suppose it could be anything. We all believe, Peter. I just happen to believe in God. (BEAT) These things… I don't think I could live in a world without God. I don't think I could stand it. (PAUSE) You?

DURING THE MONOLOGUE THE POET MOVES DOWN INTO THE LOWER PART OF THE STAGE – THE BEDROOM – IN CLEAR VIEW OF THE AUDIENCE.

THE SOUNDS OF BOMBING ARE HEARD.

LIGHT DOWN ON THE OUBLIETTE. LIGHTS UP ON THE BEDROOM.

END OF SCENE 2.

SCENE 3

THE POET PACES THE ROOM, PAUSING TO LISTEN TO THE SOUND OF BOMBING FROM AFAR, WORRIED IT'S DRAWING CLOSER.

HE CHECKS HIS WATCH SEVERAL TIMES IN CONCERN.

THERE'S A KNOCK AT THE DOOR AND HE HURRIES TO OPEN IT.

FLYING INTO HIS ARMS, SARAH BURSTS THROUGH THE DOOR. THE COUPLE KISS WORRIEDLY AND PASSIONATELY AS THEY TALK, OVERLAPPING.

SARAH   What are you doing here?

POET   I thought you weren't coming.

SARAH   It's not safe.

POET   I've come to get you out.

SARAH   (EASING) What?

POET   Out. I've come to get you out. (THE COUPLE DISENGAGE) It's too dangerous here. They're taking the capital. If they take the airport we might never get out. I've got some friends with the American Embassy…

SARAH   I thought they'd all pulled out already?

POET   Non-essentials. These are… We'd be flying out with the army, basically. But it's still under diplomatic….

SARAH   I can't just go.

POET   Of course you can. You can.

SARAH   Sandy…

POET   He'll be fine. Honestly. The missions are going to pull everyone out.

SARAH   He's not in the city.

The Visitor

POET   (FRUSTRATED) He's… I can't… Sandy's a big boy, Sarah…

SARAH   Why did you come?

POET   It's not safe, Sarah.

SARAH   I wish you hadn't come. Here of all places. I thought this time...

POET   Do you have things? Things you want to collect?

SARAH   No.

POET   Nothing?

SARAH   Nothing. I'm too tired, Peter. I'm too tired … I'll go with you. If you still want me…

POET   They want us to stay here. In the hotel. They've got people here. So we just stay put and they'll come and get us.

SARAH   We should never have come here. It's not… They're evil. I really think that. They're evil.

POET   You're shattered.

SARAH   How long can you live with injustice before you become unjust, do you think? We did good. At first. There's… There's a lot of poverty here, Peter. People have nothing. Nothing! We've failed them. Miserably. Politically, morally, we've failed them. Twenty years. That's how long they had democracy here. Free trade. (SHE LAUGHS) Twenty years and they're rejecting us completely. It's so stupid.

POET   We've got a little time.

A BOMB EXPLODES, MUCH CLOSER NOW. THERE'RE FOOTSTEPS IN THE HALL, PEOPLE SHOUTING, RUNNING. THE PAIR LISTEN.

Thomas Alexander

SARAH   In Africa…

POET   Don't worry about it.

SARAH   When I was… When they attacked us. You could understand it, you know? This was… This was how it was, with people. This was… They made their living like this. Road blocks. This little hundred metres of road. This is how they made their money. We just didn't have any.

POET   Don't think about it.

SARAH   It was my idea, you know, to go round. It was my idea.

POET   Hush.

SARAH   We had money. I don't know why I said that. We had money. But it was donation money, you know. For the school.

POET   It's over now.

SARAH   So I said, sure, drive round. I… I thought I was being so clever. We'd saved… Then… I didn't even hear it. The blast. Just… Everything was red and the truck was being thrown. You know? Like a rag. Almost casually… He was… He annoyed me so much, you know that? Always chewing this tobacco leaf. Over and over. It used to drive me crazy. And I killed him.

POET   They killed him. They did. They put the roadside bomb there. Not you. You didn't kill anyone.

SARAH   Poor Peter. You're so lost here, aren't you? Like a child really.

POET   It's you I'm worried about.

SARAH   Like a little boy. You shouldn't have to see this. Not you. I love you. You know that? I always have. Right from the very first moment. So… beautiful. Like you didn't belong to the real world.

POET　　　　I think they're getting closer.

SARAH　　　There's this boy. Kinhio. He's... You should see this kid, Peter, he's... He reminds me of you a lot. You know what I mean? He's with Sandy.

POET　　　　Then he'll be fine.

SARAH　　　You shouldn't have to see this. You should stay like you are. You shouldn't exist. Not here. Not here.

POET　　　　Sarah, I need you to listen to me now. Are you listening? We're getting out of here, alright? Whatever's happened, we're getting out of here. I promise. We're getting out of here. Okay?

SARAH　　　Yes. Of course. Yes. You always came for me. Didn't you? No matter where I was.

POET　　　　You came for me too.

SARAH　　　Really?

POET　　　　In the ways that count. Yes. You did.

SARAH　　　Good. (BEAT) Good.

POET　　　　Is there... I hesitate to ask this... is there any way to get word, to Sandy?

SARAH　　　He's out of the capital. The boy... I'm not even sure where. He was trying to get... We've got this boy, at the office, and the penicillin here is just, well... Out of date is the word, I suppose. There's this man he knows, in Kurvet. He's a trader, black market, and he thinks he can get some for us, but I have no idea where he's meeting him.

POET　　　　There's no one with a contact number?

SARAH　　　Poor Peter. No. There's no contact number. It's... He's been gone five days already but getting back into the city... You know how this thing started? The real thing, I mean, not the thing on the news. There was a car accident. Simple as that. A car accident. Minister of something or other but it was a hit and run and the government thought it was the militants, so they start cracking down and the next thing... This. Stupid, isn't it? I get hit by a roadside bomb and it's just another day at the office. A minister crosses the road without looking both ways and we're smack bang in the middle of a war.

A MOBILE PHONE STARTS TO RING FROM SOMEWHERE ON THE BED. THEY BOTH JUMP AND THE POET STARTS TO RUMMAGE AROUND, LOOKING FOR IT.

POET   Shit. They gave me this phone... (FINDING IT, HE OPENS IT AND HITS A BUTTON) Hello? (PAUSE) Right. Yes. (HE LOOKS AT HIS WATCH) Now? Okay.

HE HANGS UP.

POET   (CONT.) Do you have your passport? (SHE SHAKES HER HEAD) They want you to talk to you. In the lobby. It's just a formality. They need... It's just a formality. They know who you are but they need to meet you.

SARAH   Now?

POET   They're waiting. Come on.

SARAH   No. No. Peter. You stay. They... They'll want to ask me about Sandy. Personal things, you understand? It's better that you stay. You'll only start acting like a jealous lover and we don't have the time. You stay. I'm sure it's nothing. I'll be a couple of minutes. Are you packed?

POET   I didn't bring anything.

SARAH   I'll only be a couple of minutes. Okay?

THE VISITOR

POET   Okay.

SHE KISSES HIM.

SARAH   Okay. It's for the best.

POET   Call the room if there's any problem.

SARAH   I love you. You know that?

POET   I love you too. Call me if you need anything.

SHE TURNS FOR THE EXIT AND HE TURNS TO THE WINDOW, FOCUSING ON THE STREET OUTSIDE. SHE WATCHES HIM FOR THE LAST TIME, AND THEN EXITS.

WE HEAR THE SOUND OF THE ELEVATOR AND FOOTSTEPS HEADING TOWARDS THE DOOR.

THE POET STANDS THERE FOR A MINUTE, DISTRACTED, THINKING. THEN HIS THOUGHTS TURN BACK TO HER AND HE REALIZES SHE'S JUST SAID GOODBYE FOR THE LAST TIME.

POET   (CONT.) Sarah!

LIGHTS DOWN ON THE BEDROOM. LIGHTS UP ON THE OUBLIETTE.

THE POET – OSTENSIBLY HURRYING AFTER HER – RETURNS UPSTAGE TO THE OUBLIETTE.

END OF SCENE 3.

SCENE 4

THE DOOR OPENS TO THE OUBLIETTE AS THE POET REACHES THE STAGE.

THE JAILOR ENTERS, CHECKING ON THE TWO MEN BEFORE USHERING IN THE PROTÉGÉ, WHO PUSHES AN ELECTRIC CHAIR THROUGH THE OPEN DOORWAY.

THE MISSIONARY REMAINS CALM AND MOTIONLESS IN HIS CORNER, QUIETLY DEFIANT, BUT THE POET STEPS FORWARD QUICKLY, OPENING HIS MOUTH TO SPEAK, THE ANGER RISING IN HIM.

CALMLY BUT FIRMLY THE JAILOR HITS THE POET IN THE FACE. BLOOD EXPLODES FROM HIS MOUTH AND THE POET FALLS TO THE FLOOR, SHOCKED AS MUCH AS PAINED BY THE SUDDEN VIOLENCE.

THE PROTÉGÉ, GIGGLING, MOVES THE CHAIR TO THE FRONT OF THE OUBLIETTE, NO MORE THAN A FOOT FROM THE EDGE.

THE POET ATTEMPTS TO RISE AND THE JAILOR PUTS HIM DOWN AGAIN WITH SEVERAL SWIFT BLOWS, THE SUDDEN AND BRUTAL VIOLENCE NEVER REFLECTING ON THE MAN'S CALM FACE.

ASSURED THAT THE POET WILL NOT TRY TO RISE AGAIN, THE MAN TURNS HIS ATTENTION TO THE MISSIONARY.

THE PROTÉGÉ GRABS THE MISSIONARY WHO STRUGGLES AGAINST HIM, DRAGGING HIM TO THE CHAIR, THE WEAKENED MAN EASILY OVERPOWERED BY THE STRONGER PROTÉGÉ.

THE POET STIRS AND THE JAILOR ADDRESSES HIM WHILST SECURING THE MISSIONARY TO THE CHAIR.

JAILOR   I warned you to leave. I did tell you. Yes? I

The Visitor

read your book. Not all. But, yes. I did not like it. All this love, all this energy. Over what? A woman? How is that love? Eh? How is that right? I thought to myself, what if we all acted like this, yes? What if we were all this selfish, this… stupid. Where would we be? You love a woman. So what? Everyone loves a woman. You think this gives you rights in this world? You think this makes you honourable? But you have money, so do you help with it? Do you do good? You waste it. Waste it! On this woman. You waste words on a woman. Words, I can understand! Words cost air, but life? Money? No, this is not to be wasted.

POET   (WEAKLY) Leave him alone!

JAILOR   And then I thought. You were like the fat cats. The fat cats before the revolution! You wasted things. You wasted air and life and money on, what? Cars, gold, women? Stupid. This here. This chair is great American invention. Like you. Idea is simple.

HE NODS TO THE PROTÉGÉ WHO MAKES A CONNECTION AT THE BACK OF THE CHAIR, ELECTROCUTING THE MISSIONARY, PROPELLING HIS BODY RIGIDLY OUT OF THE CHAIR, HELD IN PLACE ONLY BY THE BRACES AT HIS WRISTS AND ANKLES.

POET   No!

THE CURRENT ONLY LASTS A COUPLE OF SECONDS BUT THE EFFECTS ARE DEVASTATING TO EVERYONE IN THE ROOM.

THE JAILOR CUTS THE POWER OFF AND THE MISSIONARY FALLS BACK INTO THE SEAT, BREATHING HEAVILY.

HE HAS NOT SCREAMED.

Thomas Alexander

THE POET, STILL ON HIS HANDS AND KNEES, HAS TURNED HIS FACE AWAY.

THE PROTÉGÉ LOOKS UNCOMFORTABLE AT WHAT HE HAS DONE.

THE JAILOR REACHES OVER AND GRABS THE POET'S HAIR, FORCING HIM TO LOOK.

JAILOR We must love one another and die. Is that it? Look. Look! This is what your love has done to the man. Look!

HE NODS AND THE PROTÉGÉ HITS THE CONNECTION AGAIN, SENDING THE MISSIONARY INTO ANOTHER SPASM.

THE POET TRIES TO REACH OUT AND IS HIT BY THE JAILOR.

THIS TIME THE TROUBLED PROTÉGÉ RELENTS ON HIS OWN AND THE MISSIONARY FALLS BACK INTO THE CHAIR CLOSE TO PASSING OUT, AND VOMITS UNCONTROLLABLY.

THE JAILOR TURNS ON THE PROTÉGÉ.

JAILOR (CONT., CALMLY) Why did you stop?

PROTÉGÉ Id ist... (SWITCHING TO ENGLISH TO COPY THE JAILOR) I didn't know how long.

JAILOR How long, I say. Okay?

POET Leave him alone.

JAILOR Leave who? The boy? The boy must be trained, yes? This is for the state, you understand? The state. We will have prisoners soon. Really prisoners. With information. You understand? The boy must learn. This is not so powerful. You understand? Like a light, yes? Nothing more. Look. (HE SPEAKS TO THE MISSIONARY) Are you

THE VISITOR

alright, Alessandro? Yes? See. He is alive. He is fine. The boy must learn. Beatings are good. Beatings and loneliness will break a man. It is not so complicated. Hopelessness and pain. In that order. That is what will break a man. But beatings. Beatings will leave a man black, yes? Like this! Some this is fine. Others, this will not do. Great American invention. Electricity.

MISSIONARY (HORSELY) Titus.

THE JAILOR IS SHOCKED TO HEAR HIS NAME AND HE LEANS FORWARD TO LISTEN, EMBARRASSED THAT THE MAN KNOWS HIS NAME.

JAILOR   Yes?

MISSIONARY I forgive you, Titus.

THE JAILOR IS ANGERED. EMOTION SHOWS IN HIS FACE FOR THE FIRST TIME.

HE STANDS BACK, THINKING, THEN HEADS TO THE POET.

JAILOR   And you. Do you, how did he say, forgive me?

POET   (BITTERLY) No.

THIS CALMS THE JAILOR.

JAILOR   Good. Good. This is good. But, the boy must learn. He is weak, aren't you boy? Yes. Weak. He likes suffering, but not pain. He likes hurting but not giving hurt. He is cruel. Cruel is not good. You must not hate. Hate is emotion. You must not hate. He is weak, yes? But we will teach him, poet. Will we not? He needs a teacher. Poet. You will teach.

POET   Go to hell.

IN ONE SWIFT MOVE THE JAILOR BRINGS HIS

BATON DOWN ON THE POET'S KNEE. HE SCREAMS IN AGONY AND WRITHES IN PAIN.

JAILOR   You will teach him. One way or the other. (HE MOTIONS TO THE PROTÉGÉ) Hold him.

THE PROTÉGÉ MOVES OVER AND GRIPS THE POET FROM BEHIND, PULLING HIM UP.

CALMLY AND WITHOUT MALICE THE JAILOR STRIKES HIM ACROSS THE FACE.

THE PROTÉGÉ PREVENTS HIM FROM FALLING AND THE JAILOR KNEELS IN FRONT OF HIM.

JAILOR   You are writer, yes? Poet?

HE NODS AT THE PROTÉGÉ AND HE HOLDS OUT THE POET'S LIMP HAND. THE POET, SEEING WHAT'S ABOUT TO HAPPEN STRUGGLES BUT IS HELD FIRM.

THE JAILOR BREAKS HIS FINGER.

THE POET SCREAMS IN AGONY.

JAILOR   Do not pass out on me, Mister Famous Poet. I need you to be a teacher now. I need you to show the boy how is done, yes? I need you to teach him about pain. About always causing pain.

HE DRAGS THE POET OVER TO THE CONNECTION SWITCH AT THE BACK OF THE CHAIR, PLACING HIS FOOT PAINFULLY ON THE POET'S HAND. THE POET WRITHES IN PAIN.

JAILOR   I need you to teach us. Teach us about causing pain, yes? Teach us!

POET   (WEAKLY) No.

THE JAILOR INCREASES THE PRESSURE ON THE HAND. THE POET SCREAMS.

THE VISITOR

JAILOR It is not so hard. Yes? A simple switch.

HE INCREASES THE PRESSURE AGAIN.

JAILOR Teach us.

POET Please!

THE JAILOR TWISTS HIS FOOT AND WE HEAR THE BONES BREAK. THE POET SCREAMS.

JAILOR No, no pleases! Teach us.

THE POET REACHES OVER AND FLICKS THE SWITCH, SENDING THE MISSIONARY INTO A SPASM.

HE DOES NOT STOP UNTIL THE JAILOR NODS.

JAILOR (TO THE PROTÉGÉ) There. See! That was teaching. Good teaching! You see? How easy it is to cause pain.

HE RELEASES THE HAND FROM UNDER HIS FOOT AND KNEELS BEFORE THE BROKEN POET.

JAILOR Now. Do it again.

THE POET OBEYS, SENDING THE MISSIONARY FAR OUT OF HIS SEAT, THE BONDS STRAINING AS HE WRITHES IN PAIN.

THEN, SUDDENLY, THEY BREAK AND THE MISSIONARY FALLS FORWARD, PROPELLED OFF THE EDGE OF THE CLIFF, FALLING TO THE BED BELOW AS THE LIGHTS FALL ON THE OUBLIETTE.

END OF SCENE 4.

SCENE 5

A SINGLE WEAK SPOT HOLDS THE MISSIONARY AS HE LIES INERT ON THE BED.

SARAH ENTERS, QUIETLY REMOVING HER SHOES SO AS NOT TO WAKE HER SLEEPING HUSBAND.

THE MISSIONARY TURNS IN THE BED, STILL ONLY LIT WITH THE SOFT SPOT, AND REACHES FOR A LIGHT SWITCH.

LIGHTS UP ON THE BEDROOM.

THE MISSIONARY IS CHANGED, HIS FACE UNMARKED, HIS DAMAGED EYE OPEN FOR THE FIRST TIME.

SARAH   Hey, sorry. I didn't want to wake you.

MISSIONARY S'ok.

SARAH SITS ON THE SIDE OF THE BED, TOUCHING HIM INTIMATELY.

HE SMILES UP AT HER.

MISSIONARY (CONT.) You just getting in?

SARAH   Go back to sleep.

MISSIONARY What time is it?

SARAH   Four. Go back to sleep. I like watching you sleep.

MISSIONARY How was your trip?

SARAH   Good. I think. The funding is secure, that's the main thing. They can even build the storage container, I think. As long as it comes through.

MISSIONARY I was writing a sermon. Must have fallen asleep.

SARAH   What's it about?

THE VISITOR

MISSIONARY I wanted to do something on Ruth. The women here…

SARAH Sandy…

MISSIONARY You okay?

SARAH Do you… I have something I need to tell you? I wasn't going to but…

MISSIONARY What's this about?

SARAH I'd… Do you remember Peter? Peter Armitage?

MISSIONARY Is he a contributor?

SARAH No. Well, yes. Sort of. I met him again. He's a poet. I think I've told you about him. We grew up together. Back home. His family had a summer house near my parents…

MISSIONARY I think I remember.

SARAH He was at the hotel.

MISSIONARY On the island?

SARAH Yes. He was giving a lecture. You know. One of those literary getaways. He's quite famous.

MISSIONARY (CAREFULLY) It's nice to catch up with old friends.

SARAH You know we used to be… Before we met… I didn't want you to find out. Accidentally. I didn't want you to…

MISSIONARY (SUDDENLY ACTIVE) I was talking with Mark, about Zambia. The school. He thinks it's a good idea. Education-wise alone, he thinks it's a good idea. They're going to hold a board meeting and look at funds, but it's exactly the kind of the thing we set the mission up for in the first place so I don't see there being a problem. He's thinking April. At the latest, April. There's all the shots and… AIDS is a problem. Not with the shots, naturally. I mean with the education. What's the life expectancy! But he thinks the council will go for it and there's so much we can do. So much we can do, you know.

SARAH   It's not important.

MISSIONARY (BEAT) It's the only thing that's important. Nothing else matters. Not you, not me. God provides for us so that we can… Nothing else matters.

SILENCE.

SARAH   I understand.

MISSIONARY We have no right to happiness. No right to it. I mean… This is what you wanted. What you asked for? Zambia? The school?

SARAH   Very much so.

MISSIONARY We have no right to happiness. There is nothing in the Bible about being happy. Nothing at all. I remember thinking… How often have you said that? How often? The people we put in front of us.

SARAH   I'm your wife!

MISSIONARY That's exactly what I mean.

SARAH   I missed you. I just… I wanted to let you know that.

MISSIONARY (GOING TO HER) Come here.

SARAH GOES TO HIM.

THE PAIR KISS CALMLY, SADLY, AND INTIMATELY. THE KISSING ACCELERATES INTO A PASSIONATE EMBRACE AND THE PAIR FALL BACK ON THE BED.

A SOFT SPOT LIGHTS THE OUBLIETTE. THE CHAIR HAS GONE. THE POET SQUATS ON THE EDGE OF

The Visitor

THE CLIFF, LOOKING DOWN ON THE LOVERS IN THE BED.

POET I don't believe you.

MISSIONARY I don't care.

POET She loved me.

MISSIONARY There are more important things than love.

POET How did she die?

MISSIONARY It was nothing... She walked in on a robbery. Of all the... There were looters. Lots of looters. When an army is invading a city there are always looters. She walked into the shop. The door was open so she probably thought it was open for business. So many shops were closed at that time. With the army coming. She probably looked at a hundred shops before she found that one. She just walked in and they shot her. Just like that. I was out of the city at the time. They were evacuating the embassies and I couldn't get back in time. So pointless. So...

POET I'm sorry... For your loss. I'm sorry for your loss.

THE TWO FALL BACK INTO THEIR LOVEMAKING.

LIGHTS FALL ON THE BEDROOM.

THE POET REMAINS WHERE HE IS, LOOKING OUT DOWN AT THE MEMORY OF THE MISSIONARY, OR PERHAPS HIS IMAGINATION.

EVENTUALLY HE STANDS AND WALKS BACKWARDS INTO THE DARKNESS.

THE SOFT SPOT FADES TO BLACK.

END OF SCENE 5.

SCENE 6

LIGHTS UP ON THE OUBLIETTE.

THE TWO MEN ARE SITTING IN THEIR REGULAR SPOTS, THE MISSIONARY MORE SLUMPED THAN USUAL.

THE POET IS TEARING A SHIRT FROM HIS BAG TO MAKE A BANDAGE FOR HIS HAND.

POET   She called me you know. After. When they'd closed the border.

THE MISSIONARY NODS.

POET   She told me she was sorry.

MISSIONARY   I wasn't there.

POET   She said. I think... She was careless. Concerned. About you. She wanted me to put pressure on... whoever... She said you were involved with the black market. She...

MISSIONARY   I know.

POET   I think it might be why they arrested you.

MISSIONARY   They played me the tape. In Kubari. Before. It doesn't matter.

POET   I suppose not.

MISSIONARY   How's your hand?

POET   Bad.

MISSIONARY   Welcome to the world.

SILENCE.

The Visitor

MISSIONARY (CONT.) You never read me any of your poetry.

POET (SMILING WANLY) I didn't want to torture you.

THE MISSIONARY SMILES.

MISSIONARY Sleep, I think.

THE POET LOOKS AT HIM AND NODS, NOTHING LEFT TO SAY. THE MISSIONARY FALLS ASLEEP. THE POET MOVES ACROSS AND COVERS HIM MORE ADEQUATELY WITH THE BLANKET.

THE PEEP-HOLE OPENS AND THE JAILOR LOOKS IN BEFORE ENTERING, THE POET'S BOOK IN HIS HAND.

ENTER JAILOR.

JAILOR You will need this, I think. Perhaps at the border.

THE POET TAKES THE BOOK SILENTLY.

JAILOR (CONT.) You fear me now. This is good. This is right. Yes?

POET What happened to the boy?

JAILOR Protégé? He is gone. Home. This is not his life. Perhaps you will feel good about this, yes? Time for you to go.

POET Let him go.

JAILOR That, I cannot do. Inspection comes. There must be body. There must be prisoner, yes? Otherwise I am not jailor, I think.

POET You don't need him anymore.

JAILOR That is not for me to decide. You wonder,

perhaps, why him? Why I use him? Not others?

POET   The thought had crossed my mind.

JAILOR   Religion is bad. It makes people strong. Strong enough to die. Not fear death. Harder to break. Harder to understand. You think this too, I think.

POET   That's no reason.

JAILOR   (SHRUGGING) Better one man than three. Other men die by now, I think. Give up. You go now. Yes? One in, one out. No more torture for him. This I swear.

POET   One in, one out.

PAUSE.

JAILOR   Ah, you poets. So romantic. You torture this man. You nearly kill him.

POET   Please.

THE JAILOR STUDIES HIM, THEN RAPS ON THE DOOR.

ENTER GUARD.

JAILOR   You are sure?

THE POET NODS. THE JAILOR MOTIONS TO THE GUARD AND HE LIFTS THE MISSIONARY TO HIS FEET, WAKING HIM ENOUGH TO WALK SLUGGISHLY BUT NOT ENOUGH TO RECOGNIZE WHAT'S GOING ON.

AS HE GOES TO EXIT THE POET STUFFS THE POEM HE WAS WORKING ON INTO THE DAZED MAN'S POCKET.

THE JAILOR MOTIONS AGAIN AND THE GUARD LEADS THE MISSIONARY OUT INTO THE CORRIDOR.

The Visitor

JAILOR   (CONT.) How is your hand?

POET   Broken.

JAILOR   I will get you something, yes? If you are to stay here. Perhaps you will write?

HE STEPS OUT OF THE DOOR, CLOSING IT BEHIND HIM.

THE POET ALONE IN THE CELL LISTENS TO THE FOOTSTEPS, THEN THE ELEVATOR.

HE PICKS UP THE BOOK WITH HIS GOOD HAND AND MAKES HIS WAY TO THE EDGE OF THE CLIFF, LOOKING DOWN AT THE DROP BELOW, TRYING TO SEE THE MISSIONARY LEAVING.

PAINFULLY BUT DELIBERATELY HE BEGINS TO TEAR PAGES FROM THE BOOK, THROWING THEM OUT ON THE WIND WHERE THEY DRIFT INTO THE DISTANCE.

POET   (SOTTO) Sarah.

HE TURNS, TAKING STEPS BACK INTO THE CELL, THEN TURNS AGAIN AND, RUNNING, FLINGS HIMSELF OFF THE EDGE OF THE CLIFF AS THE LIGHTS COME DOWN.

BLACKOUT.

SCENE 7

LIGHTS UP ON THE BEDROOM.

IT IS WEEKS LATER. WE HEAR THE NOISE OF A

Thomas Alexander

PLANE DEPARTING NOISILY FROM NEARBY.

PAUL, AN ENVOY OF THE AMERICAN EMBASSY, LEADS THE MISSIONARY INTO THE HOTEL ROOM. THE MISSIONARY, STILL PALE AND BRUISED, IS ON THE MEND, HIS EYE LARGELY HEALED.

PAUL   Here you go.

MISSIONARY Thank you.

PAUL   Not at all.

MISSIONARY I'm sorry. I… Your name. I've forgotten…

PAUL   Paul.

MISSIONARY Thank you, Paul. And please thank your embassy for me. Everyone has been…

PAUL   Not at all, sir. We're more than glad to help one of our friends. The flight doesn't leave for a few hours, sir. We're sorry about that. Flights here aren't exactly an exact science, if you know what I mean? There's a shower here if you want one, though I wouldn't bet too highly on hot water. Room service is passable though, sir. I'd stay away from anything uncooked, but the burgers are pretty good. Would you like me to order something for you before…

MISSIONARY No. No. Thank you. Thank you.

PAUL   No problem. Well, I guess I'll leave you alone. The, um, the mission has insisted on picking up the tab for this, sir, so there's no problem checking out. A car will take you directly to the plane, they'll give you a call here, and you just meet them in the lobby, alright?

MISSIONARY Thank you, Paul. You've been very kind. Very kind.

PAUL   Not at all, sir. After what you've been through… Well, I'll leave you alone.

The Visitor

PAUL HEADS TO THE DOOR AND STOPS.

PAUL (CONT.) If I can just say, sir? We're all going to miss her, sir. Mrs. Menine. These months she's been with us. Well, she's been great. I just wanted to say that. The perfect guest. She... They wanted to send her home, sir. When we lost word of you. She wouldn't go, sir. Said she'd take American citizenship before leaving the embassy. I just wanted to say that, you know. She's been... Well, she's an inspiration to us all, sir.

ENTER SARAH.

MISSIONARY Thank you, Paul.

PAUL (TURNING TO GO) Ma'am.

SARAH Paul.

EXIT PAUL.

SARAH (TO MISSIONARY) Where do you think you're going?

MISSIONARY I thought it was...

SARAH Sit! You know what the doctor told you. Let me look at you. See. You're healing already. You are healing, right?

MISSIONARY Of course.

SARAH We've got a couple of minutes. Kinhio says he'll meet us at the airport. If you hadn't... It's a miracle really, all of it...

MISSIONARY Sarah...

SARAH And when we get to London...

MISSIONARY Sarah. Stop.

SARAH Are you alright?

MISSIONARY I'm... Yes, I'm fine. I've... I've decided to

leave the mission.

SARAH　　　Well, London…

MISSIONARY　The Mission, the church, all of it. Everything. I'm… I don't think I believe in it anymore.

SARAH　　　It's only natural, after everything…

MISSIONARY　I don't mean that. I mean it. All of it. This isn't what I believe in anymore. All this.

SARAH　　　What then?

MISSIONARY　You. I believe in you. In us. I want… I want to be selfish. I want to believe in you!

ENTER PAUL, KNOCKING BEFORE ENTERING.

PAUL　　　Hi. Sorry. They're ready for you, sir.

THE PAIR RISE AND START TO COLLECT THEIR THINGS. SARAH MOVES AHEAD OF THE MISSIONARY AS THEY HEAD OUT OF THE ROOM.

PAUL　　　(CONT.) We've spoken with the press as well as we can manage it. I think they're going to leave you alone, but you should be prepared for a few flash bulbs upon landing…

EXIT SARAH AND PAUL.

THE MISSIONARY DIGS OUT THE PIECE OF PAPER THE POET GAVE HIM BEFORE HE LEFT. HE LOOKS AT IT AND THEN TOSSES IT ON THE BED.

LIGHTS DOWN ON THE ROOM.

LIGHTS UP ON THE OUBLIETTE.

WE HEAR THE POET READING ALOUD IN THE EMPTY CELL.

POET (OFF)

The Lords of Shouting and I rise early these days.

The Visitor

Ten million and one eyes looking eastward in expectation
Of the sun. Voices, voicing volumes, chasing
The sun skyward in the futile fulfilment of another dawn.
And I, waiting for a different call, the telephone still
On the bedside table, the letter undelivered, a pen
With the ink still in.

Satisfied, the Lords of Shouting retire into another
Morn, and I, to bed, belittled by another night
Where the sun never rises, the phone never rings
And my mind finds feelings in the most
Meaningful of myths.

LIGHTS DOWN.
CURTAIN.
THE END.

Thomas Alexander

BEGAT

BEGAT

Cast of Characters

AUTHORS NOTE

The cast is specifically designed so that a number of roles can be doubled. A cast of 5-6 is more than adequate.

SENUR – Mid Twenties. Accented

KARS – Early Twenties.

JUDGE – Sixties. Rich.

DIARMEN – Bodyguard. Physical. Forties

DOCTOR – Sixties. Rich.

OLD – Male. Sixties. Poor.

YOUNG – Male. Twenties. Poor.

KIFUR – Forties Poor. Accented

ANISI – Twenties/Early Thirties. Poor

SENATOR – Sixties. Rich.

YOUNG SENUR – A child. No more than ten

ANNOUNCER

SARAH (non speaking) – Forties.

ACT 1

SCENE 1

CURTAINS.

A MAN IN A WHITE SUIT STEPS FORWARD, WELCOMING GUESTS TO A LAVISH PARTY AT THE HOME OF THE JUDGE.

ANNOUNCER Congressman Taimor and Ms Senur Kafii.

LIGHTS UP ON THE HACIENDA.

A BALCONY STRETCHING HIGH OVER THE DEEP ARCHES OF THE BUILDING LOOKS OUT ON THE VAST LAWNS OF THE PRESTIGIOUS PROPERTY.

CICADAS SING FROM HIGH TREES, A CACOPHONY DROWNING OUT A DISTANT QUARTET SOMEWHERE IN THE BUILDING IN THE MIDST OF THE PARTY.

ON THE BALCONY A YOUNG WOMAN STANDS LOOKING OUT. THE NIGHT IS HOT AND HUMID. SHE IS DRESSED IN A SIMPLE SLIP OF A DRESS. A SCARF, WORN FOR PROPRIETY, HAS SLIPPED OFF HER SHOULDERS AND HANGS FROM HER ARMS AROUND HER WAIST IN THE HEAT.

SHE IS PRETTY IN AN UNCONVENTIONAL WAY, DARK AND EARTHY. SHE SEEMS AT PEACE.

KARS STEPS OUT ONTO THE BALCONY, TWO GLASSES OF CHAMPAGNE IN HIS HAND. HE IS WELL DRESSED IN FINE COTTON AND LEATHER SHOES, HIS HAIR PULLED BACK. YOUTH AND BEAUTY ARE ON HIS SIDE.

BEGAT

HE APPROACHES HER CALMLY AND HANDS HER ONE OF THE GLASSES. PAUSING SHE TAKES IT WITHOUT A WORD, AND THE PAIR OF THEM LOOK OUT INTO THE NIGHT SKY.

KARS   I liked what you said. In there.

SENUR   What did I say?

KARS   The murder. People should speak out like that more often.

SENUR   I don't think I made many friends.

KARS   And is that what you want – friends?

SENUR   We all need friends.

PAUSE.

KARS   He did it. Of course. We all know that, the bloated... Did you ever meet him? The senator?

SENUR   Is that what you came out to talk to me about?

KARS   Perhaps.

SENUR   Thank you for the champagne.

KARS   Who did you come with?

SENUR   Who said I came with anyone.

KARS   This doesn't look like your sort of party.

SENUR   Whose party is it?

KARS   Mine.

SENUR   Then it doesn't look like my kind of party. What do you imagine my sort of party would look like anyway?

KARS   Better.

SHE SMILES.

SENUR   Do you always come to your father's parties?

KARS   I have to. I live here. It's my home.

SENUR   I see.

KARS   Do you?

SHE LEANS IN AND KISSES HIM.

SENUR   Very.

HE LOOKS AT HER FOR A SECOND AND THEN REACHING OUT PULLS HER PASSIONATELY TOWARDS HIM. SHE RESPONDS, PULLING HIM IN DEEPER, THEN BITING HIS LIP STEPS BACK QUICKLY.

HE LOOKS AT HER, PAIN MAKING HIM ATTEND TO HIS LIP.

HE GLARES AT HER AND THEN, THROWING HIS GLASS AGAINST THE WALL, RUSHES INTO HER, CRUSHING HIMSELF AGAINST HER.

SHE LETS HER GLASS FALL TO THE FLOOR AND RESPONDS, THEIR PASSION RISING, GREEDY WITH EACH OTHER.

AT THE LAST MOMENT HE TURNS HER SO THAT SHE FACES OUT FROM THE BALCONY AND, LIFTING HER DRESS TO FIND NO UNDERWEAR, ENTERS HER.

AS SOON AS SHE IS AWAY FROM HIM HER FACE CHANGES FROM PASSION TO ENDURANCE.

KARS   God!

HE FINISHES, COLLAPSING ONTO HER BACK. SHE STROKES HIS HAIR.

SENUR   It's alright.

SOMETHING IS STICKING INTO HIM, SOMETHING ATTACHED TO THE BACK OF HER DRESS. HE ADJUSTS HIMSELF AND REACHES FOR IT.

BEGAT

FINDING A SMALL GUN SECRETED THERE HE PULLS AWAY FROM HER.

KARS   What's this?

HE IS STRUGGLING, ADJUSTING HIMSELF AND TRYING TO DRESS, ALL THE WHILE LOOKING AT THE GUN.

SHE IS CALM AND QUIET. SHE TAKES A STEP TOWARDS HIM. HE POINTS THE GUN AT HER.

KARS   (CONT.) No!

SHE STOPS, RADIATING CALM, AND WAITS FOR HIM TO SPEAK AGAIN.

KARS   (CONT.) Why do you have a gun?

SENUR   It's my father's. He makes me carry it. For protection.

KEEPING THE GUN AIMED AT HER.

KARS   Your father?

SENUR   When I was ... My mother was attacked. She was... He insists I carry it. For protection.

KARS   I see.

SENUR   (HOLDING OUT HER HAND) May I have it?

KARS (JOKING AROUND) And what's to stop me just shooting you now? What you said before – an injustice so obvious it beggars silence?

SENUR   It's not loaded.

KARS   Why carry it if it's not loaded?

SENUR   (CALMLY) A gun can scare people. It doesn't have to be loaded. They just have to think it is. May I have it?

KARS THINKS ABOUT IT, THEN TURNING IT HANDS

IT BACK TO HER.

KARS　　　　You shouldn't keep it there. It might fall out.

SENUR　　　(TAKING THE GUN) Thank you. Do you see any other place where I can put it? (SHE HOLDS IT, WEIGHING IT) Did I scare you?

KARS　　　　My father is… He's a judge. He works in law enforcement.

SENUR　　　And?

KARS　　　　I've seen a lot of guns.

SENUR　　　I see.

KARS　　　　I wasn't scared.

KARS HAS JUST ABOUT FINISHED DRESSING AND IS ABOUT TO CONTINUE WHEN THE MAIN DOORS OPEN AND THE JUDGE AND HIS WIFE APPEAR, LEADING THEIR GUESTS ONTO THE BALCONY, MUSIC BILLOWING OUT BEHIND THEM.

INSTINCTIVELY, WITHOUT THOUGHT, SENUR TURNS AND SHOOTS. THE FIRST SHOT CATCHES THE WIFE IN THE FACE AND SHE FALLS BACK, DEAD. NO ONE MOVES. SHE ADJUSTS AND SHOOTS THE JUDGE IN THE SHOULDER.

NOW THE CROWD SCREAMS.

LIGHTS DOWN.

END OF SCENE 1.

BEGAT

SCENE 2

CAR LIGHTS SHINE OUT ACROSS THE STAGE. A CAR COMES TO A HALT AND STOPS. CAR DOORS OPEN. TWO MEN – ONE LARGE, ONE SMALL – WALK OUT ONTO THE STAGE AND LOOK OUT AT A BUILDING OFF STAGE.

THOUGH BOTH ARE CARRYING GUNS THIS IS CLEARLY A DIFFERENT TIME, AND THEIR CLOTHES ARE OLD AND RUSTIC. THE TWO MEN ARE INDIGENOUS TO THE LAND. THEIR DRESS AND MANNERISMS BETRAY AN INCOMPATIBILITY TO THE OPULENCE OF THE PARTY.

THE TWO MEN LOOK OUT FROM BEHIND THE CAR LIGHTS. THE OLDER ONE NODS AND THE YOUNG ONE HANDS HIM HIS RIFLE BEFORE RETURNING TO THE CAR.

THE OLD MAN CALMLY RAISES HIS RIFLE IN THE AIR AND FIRES OFF A ROUND.

OLD (CALLING OUT TO THE HOUSEHOLD OFF STAGE) Might as well come out! This doesn't have to be any worse than it is. Don't want us coming in to get you.

SILENCE.

THE YOUNG MAN RETURNS TO HIM, HOLDING TWO OLD-STYLE BURNING TORCHES, UNLIT, AND A CAN OF ACCELERANT.

THE OLD MAN IS LISTENING.

YOUNG Want me to light them?

OLD Not yet.

SILENCE. THE TWO MEN LISTEN.

YOUNG What do you reckon's happening?

OLD Looking out the back, no doubt. You see a movement back there...

THEY HEAR SOMETHING THAT WE CANNOT. THEY PAUSE AND LISTEN HARD.

YOUNG What's he saying?

OLD (SHOUTING OFF) You know what we're really here for! Might as well not make it any harder on yourselves!

SILENCE AS THEY LISTEN TO THE REPLY.

OLD (CONT.) Yeah, well. He's not my god. Come on out now!

YOUNG What's he talking about?

OLD Smiting.

HE RAISES HIS GUN IN THE AIR AND FIRES AGAIN.

OLD (CONT., SHOUTING OFF) No one gets hurt! You got my word on that. Come on out now and you'll be fair treated. Word given!

THEY LISTEN IN SILENCE.

YOUNG Now?

OLD Yeah, might as well.

THE YOUNGER MAN POURS ACCELERANT ON A TORCH AND, HOLDING IT OUT, LIGHTS IT. IT FLARES UP IN THE NIGHT LIGHT, ENGULFING THE TWO IN ITS SHADOWS.

HE IS ABOUT TO LIGHT THE SECOND BUT THE OLDER MAN PUTS HIS HAND ON HIS ARM.

OLD (CONT., SHOUTING OFF) You see the way it is. Can't say you ain't had fair warning neither! Come on out now and no one will be harmed. Word of honour!

BEGAT

YOUNG   Can't barely make the back out with the light.

THEY LISTEN.

OLD   (SHOUTING OFF) This ain't something new to us! You understand me?

YOUNG   How you hear so good?

OLD   Listening.

THEY LISTEN.

YOUNG   What's he saying now?

OLD   (IGNORING HIM. SHOUTING OFF) I'm not here to debate with you. You got your reasons, same as me, but

THEY LISTEN.

YOUNG   What's they doing?

OLD   Reckon that's prayer. (HE HOLDS HIS HAND OUT FOR THE TORCH) Give that here.

THE YOUNGER MAN HANDS OVER THE TORCH. THE OLDER MAN POINTS HIS RIFLE TOWARDS THE BUILDING.

OLD   (CONT.) Run a line up, then. I've got you covered.

THE BOY STARTS TO POUR ACCELERANT IN THE DIRECTION OF THE HOMESTEAD AND SPLASHES IT TOWARDS THE BUILDING.

OLD   (CONT., SHOUTING OFF) Cold night and I ain't getting any younger! Dry enough though, I reckon. Dry enough for a dozen nights as I recall. Not sure the wood in there's gonna be any protection. Come on out now. No body's getting harmed. You got my word on that. Think of the children!

Thomas Alexander

YOUNG   That'll do, you think?

OLD   (SHOUTING OFF) Think of the women! (TO THE YOUNGER MAN) You see movement out the back, you let me know. Okay?

THEY LISTEN.

YOUNG   That's funny praying.

OLD   Wouldn't be praying if it didn't sound funny.

THEY LISTEN.

YOUNG   Gas won't last.

THE OLD MAN STEPS FORWARD AND FIRES ANOTHER SHOT INTO THE AIR.

OLD   (SHOUTING OFF) Listen now. All of you! This weren't your land! Weren't yours to build on. Not in law! Not in right! You know our customs. You know our ways. Plenty of places for prayer without you coming here, so stay or go, you've got our decision. One way or another. Stay or don't stay. I'm talking to all of you now. Young and old. You know your mind. You know our ways. You leave now and nothing's gonna happen to you, one way or another. Treated properly, and you have my word! You don't have to listen to any of them in there says different. Out front or out back, you have my word. But it's up to you!

FOR THE FIRST TIME, AS IF IN RESPONSE, WE HEAR THE SOUND OF PRAYER AND SINGING, JUST AUDIBLE AND DRIFTING ON THE WIND.

OLD   Light it.

THE YOUNG MAN DROPS THE TORCH ON THE GROUND. FLAMES LEAP UP TOWARDS THE BUILDING.

THOUGH THEY DIE OUT NEAR THE MEN IT IS

BEGAT

CLEAR FROM THE LIGHT THAT THEY HAVE TAKEN HOLD OF THE BUILDING.

YOUNG   You reckon they'll leave?

OLD   Haven't met a man who doesn't fear fire over a swift run yet.

WE LISTEN TO THE SOUNDS OF PRAYER AND SINGING GROWING LOUDER.

YOUNG   Can't see nothing in these shadows.

THE OLD MAN TAKES THE RIFLE FROM THE YOUNGER, HIS NOW BEING EMPTY, AND STEPS FORWARD BEFORE FIRING REPEATEDLY INTO THE AIR.

OLD   (SHOUTING OFF) Fire! (LOUDER) Fire!!

THE SOUND OF SINGING HAS HALTED, REPLACED BY THE SOUND OF CRACKLING FIRE BUT THE SOUND OF PRAYER IS STILL STRONG. THE TWO MEN LISTEN.

YOUNG   You figure they heard?

THE FIRE IS HIGH NOW, THE LIGHT OF IT ILLUMINATING THE MEN MORE THAN THE CAR LIGHTS.

THE OLD MAN STUBS THE TORCH OUT CAREFULLY ON THE GRASS.

THE SOUNDS OF PRAYER ON THE WIND BEGINS TO BE ACCOMPANIED BY SCREAMS, THOUGH WHETHER MALE OR FEMALE WE CANNOT MAKE OUT.

YOUNG   Think we should do something?

OLD   Like?

THE SOUNDS OF PRAYER HAVE CEASED, SCREAMS

THE ONLY AUDIBLE SOUND.

SOMETHING INSIDE EXPLODES AND THE TWO MEN HAVE TO SHIELD THEMSELVES FROM THE HEAT OF THE BLAST.

THEY LISTEN.

THE SCREAMS HAVE STOPPED.

THE FIRELIGHT DIES.

THE OLD MAN SIGHS AND PREPARES TO GO.

YOUNG   Reckon they got out?

OLD   Damnedest thing I ever saw.

THEY HEAD BACK TO THE CAR.

YOUNG   What's done is done.

THE OLDER MAN PAUSES AND LOOKS AT THE YOUNGER.

OLD   No. No. Don't reckon it is. (HE MOVES TO EXIT) There'll be blood for this.

THEY EXIT TO THE CAR.

YOUNG   Long as it's not ours!

END OF SCENE 2.

SCENE 3

A SITTING ROOM IN THE JUDGE'S HOUSE, WARM AND DECADENT. THE FURNITURE IS OPULENT AND CLASSIC, THE WALLS BOOK-LINED AND ERUDITE. THIS IS CLEARLY NOT THE CENTRAL

BEGAT

ROOM OF THE HOUSE BUT NEVERTHELESS IS BOTH COMFORTABLE AND WELL USED.

UPSTAGE ARE THE DOORS THAT LEAD ONTO THE BALCONY THAT THE JUDGE ET AL HAD ENTERED FROM AT THE END OF SCENE 1.

ON ONE SIDE IS A DOOR LEADING TO THE REST OF THE HOUSE.

CENTRE A LARGE COUCH AND SURROUNDING CHAIRS CIRCLE AN ORNATE RUG.

ON THE SOFA, UNDER A PROTECTIVE BLANKET, THE JUDGE, STRIPPED TO A SINGLET, IS BEING TREATED BY THE FAMILY PHYSICIAN WHO IS CLEARLY DRESSED FOR THE PARTY. THE JUDGE, THOUGH OBVIOUSLY IN DISCOMFORT AND PAIN, IS IN FULL COMMAND OF HIS FACULTIES AND IS CONSCIOUS WHILE THE DOCTOR REMOVES A BULLET FROM HIS SHOULDER.

A BOTTLE OF THE DAY IS CLAMPED IN THE JUDGE'S HANDS AS HE YELLS AT THE DOCTOR'S PROBING.

DOCTOR   Hold still, damn you!

JUDGE   God in heaven! It feels like you're taking a bone, not a bullet!

DOCTOR   It's surprisingly deep... There. Got it.

HE DROPS THE BULLET INTO A NEARBY GLASS.

DOCTOR   (CONT.) That makes three then, I suppose.

JUDGE   Four. The Wayan child.

DOCTOR   It's lucky it was a small calibre. The closeness of it. Anyone would think bullets weren't for killing.

JUDGE   Sarah?

THE DOCTOR, PATCHING UP THE MAN'S

SHOULDER, GIVES HIM A LOOK AND SHAKES HIS HEAD. THE JUDGE DRINKS IN SILENCE.

DOCTOR   We should leave it to the police.

JUDGE   The police! Most of them were right here at the party!

DOCTOR   The real police.

JUDGE   Did she...

DOCTOR   No. No, it would have been.... She wouldn't have felt a thing.

JUDGE   You done?

DOCTOR   For now. We need to get you to a hospital. You can keep it like that for now, but you're going to need stitches and infection...

JUDGE   Not the first time I've been shot.

DOCTOR   This isn't then. We're not young men anymore.

JUDGE   Hospitals complicate things. Police complicate things. We need to know what she knows. Where's Diarmen?

DOCTOR   He's got her downstairs.

JUDGE   Well, bring her up here!

DOCTOR   For the last time...

JUDGE   Just do it, will you? Be my friend for a minute, not my physician.

THE DOCTOR THINKS AND THEN MOVES TO LEAVE.

DOCTOR   Five minutes, then we get you to a hospital, alright?

JUDGE   Get the boy in here, too.

BEGAT

THE DOCTOR GOES OVER TO THE DOOR AND LOOKS OUT AS IF TO SHOUT. HE SEES SOMEONE OFF-STAGE AND NODS. THEY'VE HEARD EVERYTHING AND DON'T NEED TELLING.

MEANWHILE THE JUDGE DRINKS HEAVILY FROM A BOTTLE, AND REACHES PAINFULLY FOR A FRAMED PICTURE ON THE COFFEE TABLE OF HIS WIFE. HE LOOKS AT IT LOVINGLY, BUT AS SOON AS HE SEES THE DOCTOR RETURNING HE STUFFS IT BEHIND HIM DOWN THE BACK OF THE SOFA AND RETURNS TO THE BOTTLE.

DOCTOR   They're coming.

THE TWO MEN WAIT. THE DOCTOR PACES.

JUDGE   How'd you forget the Wayan boy anyway?

DOCTOR   I just did.

JUDGE   He was aiming at you!

DOCTOR   Aiming isn't shooting. (RECOGNIZING THE ERROR) Sorry.

DIARMEN ENTERS, SENUR SLUMPED UNCONSCIOUS OVER HIS SHOULDER. THERE IS BLOOD AROUND HER EAR.

A BIG MAN, DIARMEN IS OLDER BUT STILL VITAL, AND THOUGH HIS CLOTHES ARE EXPENSIVE AND HIS MOVEMENTS REFINED HE IS CLEARLY NOT UNACCUSTOMED TO VIOLENCE.

KARS ENTERS BEHIND HIM.

JUDGE   Put her in the chair.

DIARMEN DEPOSITS HER ROUGHLY IN A DINING CHAIR AND TIES HER ARMS TO THE CHAIR.

KARS   What are we doing?

Thomas Alexander

JUDGE (TO DOCTOR) Did you check her?

DOCTOR A concussion, nothing more.

KARS What are we doing?

JUDGE (TO DIARMEN) Weapons? (DIARMEN NODS) Properly this time?

DIARMEN She's clean.

JUDGE Tie her. The string's in the... (HE POINTS PAINFULLY) In there.

KARS Pa?

JUDGE (TO KARS) Get me another bottle of whisky, would you?

KARS Sir...

JUDGE I'm fine, I'll... I'm going to the hospital directly...

KARS Mother...

JUDGE I know. I'm sorry.

KARS She just shot her.

JUDGE Me too!

KARS Shouldn't we go to the police?

JUDGE This... She killed your mother, Kars! God's sake boy, she walked into our home, ate our food, drank our wine, shot your mother, and tried to kill me! What do you want me to do?! Hand her over to the authorities? Lock her up? Get her some counselling for fuck's sake? She killed your mother!

KARS Stepmother.

JUDGE What was that?

KARS She killed my stepmother!

JUDGE It's time for you to grow a pair of balls, my

BEGAT

boy. Not just a cock!

KARS   She was talking about the murder. Before. At the party.

JUDGE   Get me a bottle of whiskey, would you. The good stuff. I need a level head for this and my shoulder's killing me!

EXIT KARS.

DOCTOR   Karl...

JUDGE   It was for the... It was for the boy! Damn it, Hankle! Do you think..? It was for the boy!

DIARMEN   She's awake.

JUDGE   Yes, I know. (TO SENUR) We don't have much time. Do you hear me? Why did you do this? Come on! I know you can hear me!

DIARMEN MOVES FORWARD. SENUR OPENS HER EYES AND LOOKS AT THE JUDGE.

SENUR   I wanted to kill you!

JUDGE   Yes, well. Good luck with that. You killed an innocent woman!

SENUR   There are no innocents.

DIARMEN MOVES FORWARD QUICKLY AND STRIKES HER. THE JUDGE ADJUSTS HIS WOUNDED SHOULDER.

JUDGE   Alright, alright!

DOCTOR   I gave birth to that woman! With these hands! Innocent? There was no creature more innocent...

JUDGE   (LOOKING AT DIARMEN) Yes, well, I wouldn't go that far.

ENTER KARS.

JUDGE   You came into my home and tried to kill me. Kill my wife! (SENUR LOOKS AWAY) Alright, you came into my house and tried to kill me. Why? Why did you wait so late? Why not simply kill me when you walked in.

SENUR LOOKS AT KARS.

SENUR   I wanted you to suffer.

KARS MOVES FORWARD TO STRIKE HER BUT IS BLOCKED BY DIARMEN.

KARS   You fucking bitch!

JUDGE   Alright! Alright! Would you three please... God! Give me the whisky!

DIARMEN UNCORKS AND PASSES THE JUDGE THE NEW BOTTLE. HE TAKES A SWIG.

DOCTOR   This has gone on...

THE JUDGE WAVES HIM OFF.

JUDGE   That's better. Now... What do you know about the murder of Khadife Sedat?

SENUR   Nothing.

KARS   You lying whore!

DOCTOR   You were talking about her. Everyone heard!

JUDGE   Was she a friend of yours? Come on, you might as well tell us!

SENUR   I know nothing about her.

DIARMEN   Do you want me to...

JUDGE   In a few moments, my good friend here is going to insist I hand you over to the authorities. Even if he doesn't there were enough people who saw what you did. Word is bound to reach them, no matter how well absorbed my guests are. At least one of them is going to have the foresight to call a

BEGAT

newspaper, who in turn are going to call the authorities... So you see, no matter what crimes you've committed here, I can assure you if you know anything about the murder of Khadife Sedat then we are your best bet on surviving the night.

SENUR   I know she was murdered. I know that you were the judge in the case.

JUDGE   I am the judge in every case.

SENUR   I know you let her murderer go!

KARS   You know nothing!

JUDGE   Do you...

A PHONE RINGS BOTH IN THE ROOM AND ELSEWHERE.

DOCTOR   Your time is up child.

JUDGE   (TO DIARMEN) Take it downstairs.

EXIT DIARMEN.

ALL LISTEN AS HE LEAVES THE ROOM. THE PHONE CONTINUES RINGING. THEY WAIT. THE PHONE STOPS, HAVING BEEN PICKED UP.

KARS   I think we should...

JUDGE   Do you know who I am?

SENUR   Yes.

JUDGE   I am the high judge official. That means I oversee cases. I oversaw the case of Khadife Sedat. And yes, you're right. I threw the case out. Do you know why?

KARS   What has this got to do with...

SENUR   You got your fat friend off.

JUDGE   The senator? No. No, I threw the case out because there was no proof. Oh, there was, trust me, mountains of it, to begin with. Fingerprints, eye witnesses...

Thomas Alexander

But all of these have a habit of going away. Little by little. One by one. Senator Matgolise is a very... powerful man. Very powerful and... Well. The authorities are very corrupt. Something I thought we had taken care of but... That is the law! We make laws and we must follow them. No matter how badly people treat them.

SANUR   Are you going to torture me?

JUDGE   Probably. Does that frighten you? Like I said, there are laws. Men's laws. And there are God's laws as well, but you know which ones are most important? Men's! God's laws, well, they're perfect and perfection doesn't need help from anyone. But men's laws... I spent... Have you ever read our constitution? I spent months on it. Months! The best minds, the best men, and still it's imperfect! You see, God's laws, they are in the heart. Men's laws are made of words and words can be corrupted, so we must help them. We must help them with the truth! That's how you help words. You shine the light of truth on them and find the bits where it seeps through!

KARS   Stop it!

JUDGE   Other men have no such qualms. They don't want to shine the light of truth on things. They use words like shields. Like things to hide behind! Even words we make!

KARS   Enough.

JUDGE   My son has a kind heart but we both know, don't we? We both know that men who hide behind words will do anything to keep those words protecting them! They have the police and they have the judiciary and they will kill you. If I let them. So, you see, no matter what we think of you... No matter what you've done here.... No matter what, we....

KARS   Everyone out!

BEGAT

DOCTOR Kars...

KARS Out! Now! I want to talk to my father!

DOCTOR This is not the time...

DIARMEN RE-ENTERS. THE THREE MEN LOOK AT HIM.

DIARMEN SHAKES HIS HEAD.

DIARMEN Caterers.

KARS I mean it! OUT! Now! I need to talk to my father!

THE JUDGE LOOKS TIRED BUT HE NODS TO THE TWO MEN WHO MOVE TO GO.

DIARMEN The girl?

KARS I want her to hear this!

DOCTOR I'll see to the body.

EXIT DOCTOR.

DIARMEN You sure?

JUDGE He calls no one!

DIARMEN NODS AND EXITS.

JUDGE Pass me a glass, would you?

KARS THINKS ABOUT IT.

JUDGE (CONT.) Pass me a glass!

THE BOY ACQUIESCES AND GOES TO GET A GLASS.

JUDGE (TO SENUR) I spoil him, I know. But blood will do that. Also, his mother just died.

SENUR Stepmother.

THE JUDGE GLARES AT HER IN ANGER, THEN TAKES THE GLASS FROM KARS AND HOLDS IT OUT FOR HIM TO POUR, WHICH THE BOY DOES.

JUDGE   Say it then.

BUT KARS IS TOO ANGRY TO SPEAK. HIS HAND SHAKES AS HE POURS THE DRINK.

JUDGE   (CONT.) Don't worry about her. She'll be dead before daybreak.

KARS   How can you…? How can you! It's... She's not even dead an hour and...

JUDGE   Don't you dare! You didn't even... (HE YIELDS, SIPS HIS DRINK.) That was harsh. Shock, I suppose. The mechanism.

KARS   I know you! I know that tone!

JUDGE   Kars…

KARS   Kill her! Kill her and be done with it. Diarmen...

THE JUDGE IS SHOCKED BY THIS.

KARS   (CONT.) It's what you want. Don't deny it! (TO SENUR) You're going to die, bitch! You think...

JUDGE   Stop it! Stop it. You know that's not...

KARS   This woman...!

JUDGE   She's a girl!

KARS   Diarmen...

JUDGE   That is not what we do!

SENUR   It's what I do! If you don't have the…!

JUDGE   Shut your mouth or I'll have it shut for you!

SILENCE.

JUDGE   Kars... Listen...

KARS   What have you got her here for if not...

JUDGE   Listen....

BEGAT

KARS   No, I won't. I won't listen to any more of... (HE POINTS TO THE BOTTLE) This!

JUDGE   (LOUDLY) You will. You will! You will listen! She was my wife – mine! Stepmother? She was my wife! But... There are bigger questions here! Bigger...

KARS   I don't...

JUDGE   Matgolise is... There are holes, do you understand this? Real holes! Corruption! And... I don't know how high up it goes. I don't know how far it goes! Why do you... The reason for this party tonight was to work out where our weaknesses....

KARS THROWS THE BOTTLE ACROSS THE ROOM AND IT SMASHES ON THE WALL.

THE JUDGE RISES SHARPLY TO CONFRONT HIM.

JUDGE   We are weak! Understand me? You think someone could have come in here and tried to assassinate me... We are weak! And we are paying for it! I am trying to maint... I will have justice! In this country! And I am...

THE DOOR OPENS AND DIARMEN ENTERS, ALERTED BY THE NOISE.

DIARMEN   Is everything alright?

JUDGE SLUMPS INTO THE CHAIR AGAIN.

JUDGE   We decided to take a vow of abstinence.

KARS STORMS PAST THEM.

KARS   Do what you want but I'm telling you this! If you don't put a bullet in her head, I will!

EXIT KARS.

JUDGE   (TO SENUR) Don't mind my son. Blood will be spoilt.

SENUR   He is a playboy.

DIARMEN   What's that about?

JUDGE   The Doctor?

DIARMEN   With...

HE GESTURES. THE JUDGE NODS.

JUDGE   Good. Quickly then. Help me! Shut the door and... Try to keep your dick in your pants this time. (TO SENUR) What's your name?

SENUR   My name is Senur Kafii.

JUDGE   Do you know what is happening here?

SENUR   You want to hurt me. But you won't.

JUDGE   Don't tempt me! Did you know Khadife Sedat?

SENUR   I know you let her murderer go free.

JUDGE   But you didn't know her?

SENUR   No, I did not.

JUDGE   There's no point lying to us!

SENUR   (BEAT) I wish I had. I wish I were able to avenge her as well, but... I only know what I read in the papers. What people say in bars.

DIARMEN   She could be lying.

JUDGE   No, no. I don't think she is. So. Why are you here? Why kill me?

SENUR   There are thousands who want you dead!

JUDGE   (TO DIARMEN) Who did she come with?

DIARMEN   I don't know.

JUDGE   Her accent, her clothes... The two don't match. Did everyone sign the guest book?

BEGAT

DIARMEN. I think so.

JUDGE Check the book! I want to know who she came with.

DIARMEN She could have used a false name.

JUDGE Did you?

SENUR SHAKES HER HEAD.

JUDGE (CONT.) Check the book.

DIARMEN I don't suppose you'd save us the effort? (TO JUDGE) I can get it out of her.

THE TWO MEN LOOK AT HER.

JUDGE Check the book first. And disconnect the phones. If you haven't already.

DIARMEN First thing I thought of.

THE JUDGE NODS AND DIARMEN EXITS.

JUDGE We were never friends, you know. Matgolise and I. Conspirators, maybe, but never friends.

SENUR The corrupt die!

JUDGE Not in my experience! (PAUSE) You are not the first assassin they have sent to kill me.

SENUR Just the last!

JUDGE Shall I tell you a story?

SENUR Let me tell you one.

JUDGE Is it short?

SENUR We came to this land two hundred years ago. Three generations!

JUDGE I think you don't understand what we mean by short.

SENUR We came to this land two hundred years ago.

Thomas Alexander

Was it ours? Was it ours to take?

JUDGE   Is this irony? I hate irony!

SENUR   We came to this land two hundred years ago, and when we came to this land we owned it. We owned it. It was ours. There were no cities. There was no progression. When a swallow takes a tree for its nest...

JUDGE   Why a swallow?

SENUR   Does it care what other birds have lived in the branches? Does it look for... Remnants of nests... Twigs that indicate that a decade ago a robin blessed its branches?

JUDGE   That's a bit simplistic.

SENUR   Yesterday, then? Does it care about yesterday? Does the tree care about the woodlice that infested its bark? No. It roots them out, kills them!

JUDGE   Supremacist nonsense!

SENUR   But we come, we take the land. Own the land. Write writs of ownership. And then teach them to read these! (PAUSE) One per cent of the population...

JUDGE   We don't have time...

SENUR   Root them out! Kill them! Burn everything they have and erase them from the face of the earth. That's the way we used to do it. That's the way we were made! Inside!

JUDGE   You don't strike me as a nationalist.

SENUR   We steal their property and then we teach them what property means!

JUDGE   Let me tell you my story! There was... He was a boy. Really. No more than eight or ten and he... As part of my mandate I overseer cases... I follow up on judicial inquiries. Bad justice! So I have this boy. No more than eight or ten. Couldn't have been more than seven or eight when

BEGAT

he killed them, and he stands in front of me. A young man! A young man, guilty of the most terrible crimes, but he stands in front of me not because of what he's done but because of who he is. And who he is, is a refugee. Not black, not poor, but a refugee nonetheless. And the question before me was, did he get convicted based on what he did or based on who he was and... I had to judge. I had to look that boy in the eye and judge... Judge him! His very soul, you understand?

SENUR   What had he done?

JUDGE   He had killed his pregnant sister. I don't think he knew she was pregnant. I don't think he knew what it meant. He might even have been trying to help her... We'll never know. But I had to look into his eyes and judge... Judge his soul.... Much as I'm doing now. That was this morning.

SENUR   And? Had he?

JUDGE   He was an evil little bastard that deserved everything he got and I locked him up till he gets it. Khadife Sedat was not that. There are men of power, Senur. Men who can change your life. And we all understand that. We do, but there are bigger, bigger things than that! Bigger... If someone put you up to this…?

SENUR   No one put me up to this.

JUDGE   If someone did…

SENUR   Is that how I strike you? As an assassin? A hired gun?

JUDGE   Honestly?

SENUR   Girl with a gun? Femme fatale?

JUDGE   You are. A girl with a gun.

SENUR   Do you have a picture of her? Something you keep in your wallet, perhaps. I hear people do that. Keep pictures of loved ones in their pocket. Is that what she was to you? A loved one? Or was she some trophy? Something to hang on your arm.

JUDGE   Men don't do that.

SENUR   Was she beautiful? I never really got a good look.

SILENCE.

THE JUDGE REACHES BEHIND HIM PAINFULLY AND PULLS OUT THE PHOTO FRAME.

JUDGE   Every day. Every day. You won't provoke me, you see. Men try it every day.

SENUR   Do they all shoot your wife?

THE JUDGE STARTS TO REMOVE THE PHOTO FROM THE FRAME, WANTING TO TOUCH IT, TOUCH HER.

JUDGE   She was beautiful. Not in the way you mean, but she was beautiful. Ilsa… I was married before. Ilsa was.... on the outside. Very young. Very beautiful. It's hard being married to a woman like that. A beautiful woman. Someone you... When I... The second time...

SENUR   How did she die? Your first wife?

JUDGE   Does it matter?

SENUR   For you? (THE JUDGE NODS) Twice then women have died because of you.

THE JUDGE IS ANGERED.

SENUR   (CONT.) Hit me! Go on. I want you to hit me. Your son has more balls than you! I want you to hit me! Show me your true side!

JUDGE   Like yours?

SENUR   Look at her. Look at her! Yesterday she was

BEGAT

warmth in your bed, today she is cold on the floor! Look at her!

THE JUDGE IS CRYING. HE STROKES THE FACE IN THE PHOTO AND TRIES TO CONTAIN HIMSELF.

JUDGE   I don't... Never...

SENUR   Yesterday she was fucking your friend and now she's...

JUDGE   We... It's complicated. You don't know that.

SENUR   Everyone knows that! The world knows that. They laugh at you! Behind your back. The judge's wife! His comrade-in-arms, fucking his wife!

JUDGE   You don't know what you're talking about.

SENUR   Does it only work as a pendulum these days?

JUDGE   She was... Lonely... I...

SENUR   Aren't you glad I shot her face off?

THE JUDGE ERUPTS. HE RISES QUICKLY AND YANKS HER HAIR BACK. SHE LOOKS PLEASED.

JUDGE   You don't talk about her! You don't talk about her!

SENUR   Dead. Whore!

WITH A SCREAM THE JUDGE SCREWS UP THE PHOTO AND STUFFS IT INTO HER MOUTH. HE IS SCREAMING WORDLESS PAIN AT HER, HIS FACE AN INCH FROM HER OWN. SHE WATCHES HIM, HALF FIGHTING, HALF ENJOYING HIS TORMENT.

SHOCKED AT HIMSELF HE STEPS BACK BREATHLESS, SILENT, MOUTH OPEN. SHE WATCHES HIM CALMLY, CHEWING THE PHOTO INTO A SODDEN PULP. THEN SHE SMILES AND SPITS IT INTO HIS FACE.

Thomas Alexander

HE IS SHOCKED, AS MUCH AT HIMSELF AS HER AND STEPS FORWARD, ALMOST TENDERLY, REACHING FOR HER WITH HIS GOOD HAND.

AS HE DRAWS CLOSE SHE SPRINGS, PUSHING UP WITH HER FEET, THROWING HERSELF AT HIM. SHE HITS HIM FULL FORCE AND THEY BOTH FALL BACK, WITH HER ON TOP OF HIM. HE SCREAMS IN PAIN.

SHE BITES DEEP INTO HIS SHOULDER AND THIS TIME THE SCREAM IS INTENSE. HE IS TRYING TO PULL HER OFF BUT SHE TEARS AT HIS WOUNDED SHOULDER IN ANIMALISTIC FURY.

THE DOOR OPENS, AND THE DOCTOR AND DIARMEN RUSH IN. THE DOCTOR IS TAKEN ABACK BUT DIARMEN DOESN'T HESITATE. HE LIFTS ANOTHER CHAIR AND BRING IT DOWN ON HER HEAD.

SHE FALLS UNCONSCIOUS AS WE SMASH TO BLACKOUT.

END OF ACT 1.

BEGAT

ACT 2

SCENE 1

A HOUSE, POOR AND RUSTIC. THOUGH UNKNOWN TO THE AUDIENCE THIS IS THE HOME OF YOUNG FROM ACT 1.

IF THERE IS ANY DECORATION, IT IS SPARSE. IF ANY FURNITURE IT IS OLDER THAN THE COUPLE WHO LIVE THERE.

THERE HAS BEEN A FIGHT.

ANISI LIES CENTRE STAGE, HER POOR DRESS TORN, HER STATE DISHEVELLED, HER FACE TO THE AUDIENCE. SHE HAS JUST BEEN RAPED.

BEHIND HER KIFUR IS CROUCHED, A BLOODIED BOTTLE IN HIS HAND.

THOUGH BETTER DRESSED THAN ANISI, KIFUR IS STILL NOT WEALTHY. HIS CLOTHES SHOWS SIGNS OF WEAR AND ARE DISHEVELLED FROM THE EFFORT OF THE RAPE.

HE LOOKS LOST IN A TRANCE. ANISI, STILL RESOLUTE, MAKES NO MOVEMENT TO PUSH AWAY.

SLOWLY KIFUR SEES THE BOTTLE IN HIS HAND, REGISTERS THE BLOOD ON IT, AND TOSSES IT AWAY IN DISGUST. HE STARTS TO WIPE HIS HAND ON HIS CLOTHES AND THINKS TWICE ABOUT IT. HE SCUTTLES AWAY AND LOOKS AT THE WOMAN WHO STILL DOESN'T MOVE.

KIFUR   Do you understand. (SILENCE) I need to know if you understand.

ANISI   Yes.

KIFUR   Yes, I understand or...

ANISI   (SOTTO) I understand.

KIFUR   I didn't…

ANISI   I understand. (SILENCE) May I move now?

KIFUR   I need you to under... Yes, you can move. I.. Of course.

SHE GATHERS HER SKIRT AROUND HER BUT DOES NOT RISE.

KIFUR   (CONT.) This is not my way. It's not... I need you to understand. I need... I took no pleasure in it.

SILENCE.

KIFUR   (CONT.) This is your way. His way. My sister was.... When she was young... When we were children... My sister was. She was... Colourful. Boyish. Our father... He was not a simple man. Kind but... So there was punishment. For... Misbehaviour. Punishment. And my sister was colourful so... Punishment. It was her that decided to come here. Her faith. My father... It is not our way, you understand this? Not our... She burnt. Alive, they tell me. Burnt alive... And... It's not our way. To leave the house. Like that. In... It is not our way. A woman should be covered. We believe this and... It was her faith. You understand this? Her way. Your husband... He should be here. To answer for his crimes. He should be here. So this is your law. Your way. A wife... Taking the punishment for her husband's crimes. I am trying to....

SILENCE.

KIFUR   (CONT.) You must be cold.

SILENCE. SHE SHIFTS SLIGHTLY.

ANISI   He will kill you.

BEGAT

KIFUR   Your husband?

ANISI   He will kill you.

KIFUR   I am following his law.

SILENCE.

KIFUR   (CONT.) You told me your name. I don't remember it. I should know your name. Was it... Anisi?

ANISI   He will come and he will kill you.

KIFUR   He killed my sister. Burnt her alive.

ANISI   He will kill you.

KIFUR   This isn't... This is the law! Not my law! This is how you judge yourselves. I didn't... Foreigners invade your lands? Burn them! A husband breaks the law, his wife... I didn't want to do this! I didn't want to... This is your law! He killed... My sister... He should have been here! For justice! I didn't want to do this!

SILENCE. SHE IS SHIVERING, PERHAPS FROM THE COLD, PERHAPS FROM BLOOD LOSS, BUT STILL SHE IS RESOLUTE.

KIFUR   (CONT.) It is, it's cold in here. I don't know if there are... You shouldn't be cold.

SILENCE.

HE MOVES CLOSER TO HER. SHE PREVENTS HERSELF FROM FLINCHING. PREVENTS HIM FROM SEEING HER FLINCH.

KIFUR   (CONT.) Are you cold? I don't... I don't want to...

SOUNDLESSLY HE MOVES IN AND EMBRACES HER, WARMING HER.

IT IS NOT SEXUAL, BUT IT IS COMPASSIONATE. HE

Thomas Alexander

IS CAREFUL NOT TO GET HIS BLOOD STAINED HAND ON HER CLOTHES.

NOW HER FACADE CRACKS, HER RESOLUTION GONE, STRIPPED AWAY BY THE INTIMACY, THE TENDERNESS OF THE MOMENT. HER STOICISM IS STRIPPED AWAY AND UNSEEN BY KIFUR SHE SCREAMS SILENTLY IN TERROR.

OFF-STAGE WE HEAR THE MIRRORED SOUND OF SENUR, SCREAMING IN PAIN.

END OF SCENE 1.

SCENE 2

WE ARE BACK IN THE ROOM AT THE JUDGES HOUSE. SENUR IS STILL TIED TO THE CHAIR AND DIARMEN HAS JUST RIPPED HER FINGERNAIL OUT. SHE IS SCREAMING IN AGONY.

ON THE OTHER SIDE OF THE ROOM KARS WATCHES UNCOMFORTABLY, CLEARLY DISTURBED BY WHAT HE IS SEEING.

KARS   Shit!

SENUR LAUGHS AND SPITS IN DIARMEN'S FACE. HE SLAPS HER BACKHANDEDLY, AND THE CHAIR TOPPLES OVER.

KARS   (CONT.) Shit!

DIARMEN MOVES TO PICK HER UP.

DIARMEN   She tried to kill your father. Twice! She already killed your stepmother. Would you have me read poetry?

BEGAT

SENUR   Is that it?

KARS   (ANGERED INTO ACTION) Why are you here? Who sent you!?

SENUR   (TO KARS) Little boy with a little cock!

DIARMEN LEANS IN AND SQUEEZES THE FINGERNAIL HE JUST PULLED OFF. SHE SCREAMS.

KARS   You came with Taimor. What does he have to do with this? What does he have to do with you?

SENUR   I work with him.

DIARMEN   How?

SENUR   How?

KARS   What are you doing to us?

SENUR   What does it look like? I'm destroying you! His lover. Your father! His career! All of it. I'm destroying your whole family. (BEAT) Tell me, has it started to itch yet?

KARS IS TAKEN ABACK. DIARMEN ROUNDS ON HER.

DIARMEN   Suddenly you're talkative, is that it? Good! Then talk to me. You understand? (SILENCE) You came with Taimor. He is working with Matgolise. I have a couple of questions for you. There are nine more fingers. Ten more toes. Questions and answers. Alright? I am not the judge. Understand?

SENUR   I understand.

HE CLAMPS THE PLIERS ONTO ANOTHER FINGERNAIL.

DIARMEN   Good. What is the connection between Matgolise and Taimor?

SENUR   Nothing.

HE YANKS OUT ANOTHER FINGERNAIL. IT'S HARD.

EXCRUCIATING. SHE SCREAMS.

KARS   Whore! Fucking... whore!

DIARMEN   (TO SENUR) Hey! Hey, do not pass out on me! Come on! Do you understand me? Do not pass out!

KARS   Fuck!

SENUR   Yes.

DIARMEN   Yes?

SENUR   Yes, there is a connection.

DIARMEN   Between Matgolise and Taimor? Answer me! What connection. Hey! Hey! What connection?

SENUR   (MOTIONING TO KARS) Ask him.

DIARMEN   What? What does that mean?

KARS   The... you lying whore!

SENUR   Ask him who his lover is!

DIARMEN   Enough. The senator is in on this. He will be brought to justice! They will all be. However many of them! Now, tell me what I need to know!

SENUR   (TO KARS) Have you pissed yet? Tell me.

DIARMEN   How many people in the Senate? How many of them knew about the attack! Tell me and I will spare your life. Tell me and I promise you! A day in court. I promise you!

KARS SCRATCHES HIMSELF.

SENUR   There! It itches! Tied to a chair I am beating you!

DIARMEN   What is she talking about?

SENUR   Little boy, little cock!

KARS IS WHITE NOW.

DIARMEN   Kars? What is she talking about?

BEGAT

SENUR (TO DIARMEN) Tell me, are there any cuts on your hands?

DIARMEN LOOKS AT HER BLOOD ON HIS HANDS AND WIPES THEM QUICKLY. HE ROUNDS ON KARS.

DIARMEN What did you do?

KARS It wasn't like that.

DIARMEN LOOKS AT SENUR, THEN AT KARS. HE BEGINS TO WIPE HIS HANDS OBSESSIVELY.

DIARMEN You stupid little boy!

KARS It wasn't like that.

DIARMEN Wasn't it? Yes, I'm sure you put up an extensive fight!

KARS Oh God!

SENUR Tied to a chair!

DIARMEN Quickly now. How do you know her?

KARS I don't. I.... She... We met here. At the party!

DIARMEN Just like that?

KARS She was on the balcony and...

DIARMEN And you didn't know her before?

KARS No, never!

DIARMEN I mean you'd never met her before?

KARS No. I swear it.

PAUSE.

DIARMEN Just like that. You fuck her. Just like that?

KARS On the balcony. She...

DIARMEN Alright. Alright! God.

SENUR Little boys playing.

DIARMEN Well, if you didn't know her... We… Look,

we'll get you tested but...

SENUR LAUGHS.

KARS Little bitch!

DIARMEN Kars. KARS! It's.. She's probably... You're fine! You hear me. There's no reason to think she's got...

SENUR But I do! All of it! I made sure of it! I...

KARS (DESPAIRING) Argh!

DIARMEN Listen to me. Listen! I need you to... You've got blood on you. See. Blood!

KARS It's mother's.

DIARMEN Well, let's be sure of it, shall we. Go wash it off.

KARS God... What if I...

DIARMEN Wash it off. Take a shower. Have you taken one since you... No, alright. Go take a shower. Yes? Leave this one to me, alright? Kars! Take a shower!

KARS Right. Yes. Yes, you're right.

DIARMEN Go. Quickly now.

KARS You're... Right.

DIARMEN Change your clothes.

EXIT KARS.

SENUR Run little boy!

DIARMEN TURNS AND PULLS A CHAIR UP IN FRONT OF SENUR BEFORE SITTING.

DIARMEN Just you and me now. No parlour tricks. Just little bits of truth, alright?

SENUR You won't be pulling any more nails though, will you!

BEGAT

DIARMEN   You really think I have to touch you? Is that what you think? (PAUSE) During the war there was this man. A general. And… He didn't want to face what he had done. To the people. So, I tracked him to this cave. High… Long time. I followed and followed. Really high! Right on the border. And he hid. In this cave. He had food and he had water, and I suppose he thought I wouldn't see him there. Wouldn't track him. Pass him by. So, he hid. (PAUSE) I had six shots. Seven at best. You wouldn't think it but bullets are very hard to come by in a war. That's all I had. Seven at best. And I told him. I called into the cave and I told him. Told him exactly what I am telling you here now. That I am a patient man! And… Every time he came out, I put a bullet in him. Not a death shot. Not to kill him. A nick. Just to drive him back into the cave. Seven bullets. Maximum. And him with all that food! But I didn't want to shoot him. I wanted him to suffer. The way we suffered. Seven bullets. And still he starved to death!

SENUR   You were there, weren't you? That day. I'd forgotten it until now. I could only remember his face but it was you, wasn't it?

DIARMEN   What do you do for Taimor?

SENUR   I don't do anything for him. I fetch papers, answer the telephone…

DIARMEN   What do you mean?

SENUR   I work at his office. Assisting.

DIARMEN   I don't believe you.

SILENCE.

DIARMEN   (CONT.) Why would a senator bring an assistant to one of these things?

SENUR   To impress her. To impress her because she is young and he thinks she is pretty and…

DIARMEN   I don't believe you.

SENUR   It happens all the time.

DIARMEN   What happened with the boy?

SENUR   I killed him.

DIARMEN   Why hasn't he called? The senator? Taimor. Why hasn't he called? We all saw you. We all saw you... He would have called. If this was all innocent. He would have called!

SENUR   She had a pretty face. Did you like to kiss her face? Before I blew it off.

DIARMEN   Why hasn't he called?

SENUR   Did you flinch from it? When you saw it? After. That face you kissed. Would you kiss it now?

DIARMEN   How many people? Who is coming for us? Why? Is the hospital safe?

HE RISES AND GOES TO THE PHONE.

DIARMEN   (CONT.) If I call him now. If I make a call. Will he tell me? Pretty girl he's trying to impress. Will he say that?

SENUR   You unplugged the phone.

DIARMEN   I am a very patient man.

SENUR   Why do you work for him? Still. After all these years, why do you still work for him?

DIARMEN   I can wait forever!

SENUR   It was her, wasn't it? You loved her. She loved you. (NODDING TO THE DOOR) Is he even his?

CALMLY AND WITHOUT FUSS HE UNHOLSTERS HIS GUN AND PLAYS WITH IT.

DIARMEN   How many? Who? Why?

BEGAT

SENUR   All those years and you still stayed with him!

HE RISES AND CALMLY POINTS THE GUN IN HER FACE.

DIARMEN   I won't repeat it.

SENUR   You looked just like that. Just like that! I thought it was him but...

DIARMEN   Last...

A POWERFUL SHOT RINGS OUT. AN OBJECT NEAR SENUR'S HEAD EXPLODES. BOTH DIARMEN AND SENUR FLINCH.

KARS ENTERS, A SHOTGUN IN HIS HANDS. IT IS LARGE AND UNWIELDY AND HE IS WALKING TOWARDS THEM, STILL DRESSED IN THE SAME CLOTHES AS BEFORE BUT WITHOUT HIS JACKET.

HE IS BARELY ON THE STAGE WHEN DIARMEN, ACTING COMPLETELY ON INSTINCT AT THE SOUND OF THE GUNSHOT, TURNS AND SHOOTS HIM IN THE CHEST.

THE BOY LOOKS SURPRISED AND SHOOTS WILDLY INTO THE CEILING BEFORE FALLING DOWN.

DIARMEN   Kars!

HE RUSHES OVER TO THE BOY AND PRESSES AGAINST THE WOUND.

DIARMEN   (CONT.) Kars!

KARS TRIES TO SPEAK BUT HE CAN'T BREATHE. HIS ARMS FLAP AT HIS SIDES.

DIARMEN   (CONT.) Kars! Stay with... KARS! We'll...

BUT THE BOY IS DEAD.

SENUR IS RECOVERING FROM THE SHOTGUN

BLAST NEXT TO HER HEAD.

DIARMEN   (CONT.) Kars.

SENUR   Blood for blood.

DIARMEN   Shut up.

SENUR   I killed a woman today!

HE TURNS AND POINTS THE GUN AT HER.

SENUR   (CONT.) I was aiming for a man, but I guess no one is a good shot in this house.

HE LOWERS THE GUN ONCE MORE AND TURNS TO KARS.

SENUR   (CONT.) Just a boy, wasn't he. Just a stupid, young... I killed a woman today. I didn't mean to. I was aiming for the man. Perhaps I should have been aiming at you. You loved her. His woman. Did you love him too?

DIARMEN   No.

SENUR   I meant her husband. Did you love him? (PAUSE) When I was young... I saw someone shoot a man. He was kneeling. Kneeling with the back of his head to me, like you are now. On a carpet like you. In his house. The man who killed him, he held a gun at his side, casually, like you are now. No weight in it. No... Just his hand, natural as anything. Like a stopped pendulum. Then he just swung it up, swung it up as if it had no meaning. Swung it like an arc needs an apex, and at the height of the swing he let it take the top of the man's head off. As if the two were unconnected. As if it was simple displacement. I watched. I watched like I watch every night as the top of the man's head dissipates. I watch as the body falls to the floor and every time – every time – I think the body is going to put a hand out. Arrest it. Because. That's what bodies do. That's what we've seen them do a thousand times.

BEGAT

They put a hand out. When they fall, they put a hand out! And that's how you tell when someone is dead. That's how you gauge it. You know they're dead if they can't be bothered to save themselves. I watched that man. I watched you. Doing that. Every night. Like I watched that boy die. Like I watched your woman die. And all I can think is how much better for everyone, how much better... If he had just let the arc continue and... A dead man never tries to stop himself...

DIARMEN RAISES THE GUN, AND IN ONE FLUID MOVEMENT SHOOTS HIMSELF.

AS HE DOES WE SMASH TO BLACKOUT.

END OF ACT 2.

ACT 3

SCENE 1

THE SITTING ROOM.

MOMENTS BEFORE SENUR HAS BEEN UNTIED, THE ROPES STILL STREWN AROUND THE CHAIR. SENUR IS SITTING ON THE SOFA WATCHING THE DOCTOR AS HE ATTENDS TO THE WOUNDS ON HER HANDS.

HE HAS OBVIOUSLY JUST FREED HER.

THE BODIES OF THE TWO MEN HAVE BEEN REMOVED.

DOCTOR   Does that hurt?

SENUR   It's fine.

DOCTOR   It's lucky they... You could have been tied like that for days.

SENUR WATCHES HIM, TOUCHED BY HIS KINDNESS.

THE DOCTOR SEES AN OLD MARK ON HER ARM AND STOPS. SHE DOESN'T PULL AWAY

DOCTOR   When was this?

SENUR   It's very old.

DOCTOR   It was well cut. We see a lot of these. With young people. In the hospitals. We see a lot of these. Young women who have... You knew what you were doing. Most people... We usually only see these on dead people.

SENUR   Have you ever been to a maze, doctor?

DOCTOR   Of course.

SENUR   One of those high... I went to one, once. A

BEGAT

boy where I work... He was kind and... I think he thought it would be fun. Perhaps I was to lean on him. Perhaps that was the point of it. Silly girl being led by her gallant knight to safety.

DOCTOR   I have trouble seeing you in that role.

SENUR   So did I. The hedges were... It was new. That's what it said anyway, but the hedges were high, too high to see over and... Whoever built it had a very good mind, because you'd turn and turn but no matter what you did, you'd find yourself blocked. Even if you went back on yourself, you'd find your way blocked. And eventually, eventually you just wanted to rip through a wall. Just rip through it. Cheat. Climb over it or... That's what it's like to be a girl. Young. Eventually you just get tired of being blocked. I wouldn't worry about it.

PAUSE.

I suppose... With older mazes it gets easier to find your way around. You simply follow the most worn... I suppose you wish I'd succeeded.

DOCTOR   Why would you say that?

SENUR   I killed three of your friends today.

DOCTOR   Tied to a chair? No, I'm not glad you didn't succeed. I'm a doctor. We take vows.

SENUR   You are the family doctor?

DOCTOR   I gave birth to the boy. His mother – stepmother – as well.

SENUR   Was he his son? The bodyguard?

DOCTOR   Why would you say that? There that will hold. For now.

SENUR   What will happen to me?

DOCTOR   (PAUSE) You'll go to prison. I'm sorry but...

Thomas Alexander

The police know you are here. There will be a trial of course but....

SENUR   It won't end.

DOCTOR   It never does. Life. (PAUSE) Why did you think he was Diarmen's son? The bodyguard's?

SENUR   I thought maybe...

DOCTOR   There's a lot you don't know. About us. About this family. You should know it. All of it. For what you've done here.

SENUR   It's not important.

DOCTOR   It's impossible, you know. To judge someone. To know someone. And yet that's what we do. Doctors. Judges. We never truly know and yet we have to get on with it anyway. Diarmen... He was in love with Sarah. Always in love with her. They knew each other, went to school together. But... They were separated, as young people. Lovers, I presume. They were separated by the war. I don't know the details, but they lost contact. Perhaps they couldn't... When the judge met Sarah, he'd never met Diamen. Not then. Not until a few years ago. The... Kars was already three when he married Sarah. I delivered him myself. This was his first wife. At the beginning of the... troubles. The judge had...

SENUR   You're wrong.

DOCTOR   I'm not.

SENUR   They knew each other! The bodyguard! During the war!

DOCTOR   No. The judge was overseas when the baby came. The embargo... He wasn't supposed to be but... There were complications and... She died. In this house. So when he met Sarah....

BEGAT

SENUR	They knew each other!

DOCTOR	Any... No! Diarmen. The judge. He'd never even met Sarah before. Anyway, a few years after this. After the war. The judge is hiring. All departments. Let me finish! He's been put in charge of reforming the judicial sector, and that makes enemies. There was an attempt on his life. In the courthouse. So, they hire protection. Not even the judge, this is all done for him. And who do they hire but Diarmen! The one who got away! The lovers separated by war! It was all just coincidence. They'd each thought the other dead. Nothing more.

SENUR	You're wrong.

DOCTOR	I'm really not.

SENUR	You are!

DOCTOR	Why? Tell... Tell me why it matters? Because you feel responsible? Because you think killed a man whose only crime was being in love? You didn't. I saw the bodies. I saw the...(HE POINTS AT THE RESULTS OF THE SHOTGUN BLAST) Whatever you think, whatever you... did. Today. You were not responsible. Not for that. It's not only girls who can't find the way out.

SENUR	They knew each other. Years before. During the war! The judge!

DOCTOR	No.

SENUR	They did.

DOCTOR	Senur...

SENUR	Before. In the war!

DOCTOR	I promise you...

SENUR	One night... One night. They! The judge. His bodyguard! They came to the house of a man. They came to the house of a man and killed him! There on the floor, while his family watched. They killed him! Shot him in the head and moved on. I know this!

DOCTOR   No.

SENUR   I saw it!

DOCTOR   I know. I know. I know who you are, and I'm telling you you're wrong!

SILENCE.

DOCTOR   (CONT.) Not at first. I'll admit it. Not at first but I recognized...

SENUR   How could you?

DOCTOR   Revenge is rarely...

SENUR   This isn't revenge!

DOCTOR   No? What is it, then?

SENUR   This is justice! A murderer...

DOCTOR   Sarah – the judge's wife – didn't murder...

SENUR   She was an accident!

DOCTOR   And the boy?

SENUR   (PAUSE) I wanted him to suffer. I wanted... My father was killed right in front of me! I wanted... Justice. An eye for an eye. I wanted him to regret me. I wanted him to remember me. Forever. I wanted him to remember wanting me forever! How it felt to be inside the woman who killed his... Like that man was inside me! In my mind. Every night!

DOCTOR   No one was... You weren't even there. You were just a child.

SENUR   In my mind. In my dreams, every night! Everything! That is the punishment. That is the crime! A young girl! Her father killed in front of her... I don't care what

BEGAT

you say! That man…

DOCTOR He wasn't there.

SENUR I remember him!

DOCTOR I know. I can see that. But he wasn't there. To my knowledge he wasn't even in the country. I promise you.

SENUR It was justice. Life for life! Destruction of destruction!

DOCTOR No.

SENUR How can be so sure?

DOCTOR You… So little. I remember you. Sitting there. On the floor. When … I haven't thought about that night in… Well, I guess twenty years.

SILENCE.

DOCTOR Are you going to kill me now? I wouldn't mind. (PAUSE) Well, I would. But if it was someone...

SENUR I don't believe you.

DOCTOR It was the only thing to do. Believe me.

SILENCE.

SHE LOOKS AT HIM.

SENUR I'm not going to kill you.

DOCTOR Well then. (RISING) I'm sorry. For all this. I shouldn't have…

SILENCE.

DOCTOR (CONT.) The police will be here in... You could escape, I suppose. I suppose... There's no one to stop you. Still...

HE GOES TO THE DOOR.

DOCTOR What was your real name? It was... I know it's not Senur... I just can't... She… Well, I suppose it doesn't matter.

THE DOCTOR NODS AND EXITS.

SENUR SITS SILENTLY FOR A WHILE AND THEN GETS UP, GOES TO THE FRENCH DOORS AND OPENS THEM ONTO THE BALCONY. SHE STEPS OUT AND CLIMBS ONTO THE RAILING, CONTEMPLATING JUMPING.

SHE STAYS LIKE THAT FOR A MOMENT. THE JUDGE ENTERS, HIS ARM IN A SLING. HE LOOKS TIRED AND DRAWN. HE GOES AND POURS HIMSELF A DRINK BEFORE ADDRESSING HER.

JUDGE   I'd appreciate it. If you're going to jump, I'd appreciate it.

SHE IS SURPRISED TO HEAR HIS VOICE AND HAS TO CATCH HERSELF.

JUDGE   (CONT.) It would make things so much cleaner. I'd push you myself but I think the more distance between my arm and your teeth the better.

SENUR   I'm not going to hurt you.

JUDGE   My son is dead. So... (PAUSE) Drink?

HE HOLDS OUT A GLASS. SHE COMES DOWN OFF THE VERANDA AND LOOKS AT HIM. HE PLACES IT ON THE TABLE AND STEPS AWAY. SHE APPROACHES IT LIKE AN ANIMAL.

JUDGE   (CONT.) You are supposed to love your children, you know that? It's one of those preordained things. Like sunrises. The dirty secret most of us carry is we wouldn't even invite them to a dinner party if we didn't have to. Ignore me. I'm in shock. Or something I suppose. Why is my son dead?

BEGAT

SENUR   He tried to shoot me.

JUDGE   Why?

SENUR   He... slept with me.

JUDGE   With you?

SENUR   I slept with him. Before. At the party.

JUDGE   I see. I'm obviously in the wrong rooms at my own parties. I'll ask again. My wife. The man who loved her. I have mixed feelings about that, but my son? My son! What had he ever done to you?

SENUR   You killed my father.

JUDGE   Yes. Yes, the doctor explained everything. At the hospital. He thought he recognized you. Still, I suppose I see the... Juxtaposition. In your head at least.

SENUR   Every day... Every day!

JUDGE   Yes, I know. I said I understood. (HE SIGHS) There was this woman. In court. In court you understand, everything is heightened, everything is... She was... I don't remember what she was there for. What she was doing there. I don't even remember what I said to her. It was... Something snide no doubt. Something challenging. To me, nothing. But to her.... Anyway, she... First there were letters. From her. Then letters to the papers. Again it was never truly clear what I had done but... (PAUSE) When I was a boy my father would never allow me in his library. Never allowed in there. First thing I did when he died... I went into the library and burnt his books. Not the same I suppose. You'll have to excuse me. The painkillers.

SENUR   My father was a good man.

JUDGE   I'm sure he was.

SENUR   And you killed him.

Thomas Alexander

JUDGE   We did. Yes. It wasn't personal. You know, the worst of them... I've had people through my courts. Really bad people. People who have committed... Child molesters. Rapists! People who have killed... And each and every one of them has had someone, someone who will stand up in court and tell you what a good person they are. Deep down. If nothing else we've become incredibly apt at fooling people.

SENUR   Like you, you mean?

JUDGE   Probably. And this was nothing to do with the senator? No night of the generals?

SENUR   Would you be alive if it were?

JUDGE   No. No. I suppose not. I am, it seems, an old woman in a court house. Shouting.

SENUR   When you shot my father...

JUDGE   When you shot my wife!

SENUR   When you shoot me!

THE JUDGE PULLS A GUN OUT OF HIS SLING.

JUDGE   This? Yes. I'm not sure. It was Diarmen's. The one I suppose... The doctor has promised to leave us alone. Until the police get here.

HE PUTS THE GUN DOWN ON THE TABLE AND POURS HIMSELF A DRINK. SENUR EYES THE GUN CAREFULLY.

JUDGE   (CONT.) He was a good man. Diarmen. A good counsellor. One cannot legislate the heart. I've tried. Or fate come to that. You can't legislate it. The doctor tells me you think tonight... Justice.

SENUR   I thought he was there.

JUDGE   Diarmen?

SENUR   The night you...

BEGAT

JUDGE   You thought he was with me?

SENUR   I thought that's why…

JUDGE   Why he killed himself? He did kill himself, I take it. You don't seem the type for… No… Yes. We'll never know, I suppose. Not really. But I'd guess it had something to do with honour. It usually does. Honour and love.

SENUR   How could you put up with…

JUDGE   The betrayal? No. People are more complicated than that. Much more. (PAUSE) I'd like to tell you about your father. If that's alright with you? I don't mean… Maybe we'll wrestle for the gun. Maybe I'll get tired and just shoot you. Maybe you'll shoot me. But I'd like to. Tell you. About your father. If it's something you want.

SILENCE.

JUDGE   (CONT.) Your father had a sister. I don't know if he ever… No. Well, I didn't know him. Not even of him. He wasn't from here. Not originally. But I suppose you know that. I wondered, at the time, why he stayed here. Why not just… leave. I don't suppose you'd tell me? No? No, I doubt you even know. Not really. (PAUSE) We lost ten thousand that first year. That's what ethnic cleansing does. What it's like. There is no hatred more natural than for those not like us. And we knew why. We knew the catalyst. But a… A friend. Of your father's… You are too young to remember the war. Not really. And it wasn't the best way, but it had to be done. And if I had to do it all over again…. There are times when justice has to be dragged into the street, and there are times it's better behind closed… (HE DRINKS) People kill people. Not ideals or money. People. And we will do it for the slightest excuse. I think it scares us. Life. I think we can't look at it properly. So big and so vast. Endless from our perspective. So we create…

Laws. Reasons. God's and man's. Put us on one side of it and others on another and ask everyone to... get along. There are more cock-eyed ways of punishing a person than there are of anything else. I'm old. And stupid. And maybe I was wrong. But we'd barely started to get it stopped when we found out it was your father. (HE DRINKS AGAIN, EXHAUSTED) I'm tired. I think. They gave me something for the pain. I said I'd shoot you if I was tired, didn't I? Still. (HE PAUSES) I think I'll go to bed instead.

HE RISES. SHE ALMOST MOVES TO HELP HIM.

JUDGE   (CONT.) Be so good as to wait here for the police, would you.

HE GOES TO THE DOOR.

JUDGE   (CONT.) I miss my son. (PAUSE) Will that be enough, do you think?

SILENCE.

JUDGE   (CONT.) Good night, child.

HE EXITS. SHE SITS THERE, THE GUN NEAR HER. WE WAIT. LIGHTS START TO FADE. WE SEE THE FLASH OF POLICE LIGHTS. SHE REMAINS STILL.

FADE TO BLACKOUT.

END OF SCENE 1.

SCENE 2

THE JUDGE'S OFFICE AT THE LAW COURTS DAYS LATER.

BEGAT

THE JUDGE HAS JUST RETURNED TO HIS OFFICE FROM COURT. PAPERS ARE STREWN ACROSS HIS DESK. HE SLOWLY SLIDES HIS ROBE OFF, CAREFUL OF HIS STILL PAINFUL SHOULDER, AND HANGS IT UP.

THERE IS A KNOCK AT THE DOOR.

JUDGE   Come.

THE DOOR OPENS AND SENATOR MATGOLISE ENTERS.

SENATOR   There was no one outside.

JUDGE   Come in. No, no one outside. I didn't think either of us wanted any chance of this conversation being overheard, senator.

SENATOR   I see. I was sorry to hear about your son. Your wife too, of course.

JUDGE   Thank you.

SENATOR   Such terrible times we live in. In your own home, too. Just... shocking!

JUDGE   Have a seat senator.

SENATOR   It's a good thing I wasn't invited. To the party, I mean. I shudder to think....

JUDGE   I wanted this chance to talk.

SENATOR   I'm guessing this isn't about judicial overview, then.

JUDGE   No. And I'm sorry about the subterfuge.

SENATOR   She was an ex-convict, I hear. The assassin. An ex-convict. A... custodian of these courts.

JUDGE   No. No, she wasn't.

SENATOR   Is that right? Well. Guess we can't believe

what we read in the papers these days after all.

JUDGE   I suppose not.

SENATOR   I'm just saying. Nothing you hear or see is the truth.

JUDGE   Isn't it?

SENATOR   I'd believe you know that better than anyone... Judge. I'm just saying, because if I've been dragged in here for a scolding. I...

JUDGE   A scolding?

SENATOR   Out of respect for your family...

JUDGE   A scolding? Senator. I'm not sure...

SENATOR   I was hoping you were calling me down to build bridge....

JUDGE   Khadife Sedat. It helps to say her name out loud.

SENATOR   Be careful what you're insinuating, judge.

JUDGE   I'm insinuating that you raped and killed Khadife Sedat. I'm insinuating that you invited her to your home. I don't care why. And that when she tried to leave, you forcibly raped her and strangled her in your own living room.

SENATOR   Out of deference to the dead...

JUDGE   Fuck the dead. I'm insinuating that you bribed police officials. Made or helped make evidence disappear, and put pressure on the newspapers to cover it up.

SENATOR   (RISING) If that's all you...

JUDGE   Sit! Down! (BEAT) Didn't matter to you that she was a child. Maybe that helped. I'm not one to judge. No, wait. That's exactly what I am! It didn't matter that she was a child! It didn't matter that she was poor, uneducated...

BEGAT

SENATOR   Well! I would think you of all people...

JUDGE.   I of all people would... What?

SENATOR   Didn't you just have your own little run in with a native girl?

PAUSE.

JUDGE   Senator, do you know what the party was for the night of...

SENATOR   I know I wasn't invited.

JUDGE   No. No, it was a party to see if I still held any sway. To see if I still had any clout. Enough to take you down. Police, press, decision makers... I wanted to know just how many you had in your back pocket.

SENATOR   And how'd that go for you?

JUDGE   This country hangs by a thread. A literal thread!

SENATOR   What's it made of – horse shit?

JUDGE   Justice! I've always believed that. If justice can be done… If justice can be seen to be done then...

SENATOR   Like I said. Horse shit!

JUDGE   We lost... thousands. In the war. Tens of thousands. Both sides. The sheer...

SENATOR   We'll agree to disagree on that.

JUDGE   The numbers?

SENATOR   The loss!

SILENCE.

JUDGE   I want you to resign senator.

SENATOR   No.

JUDGE   Just like that?

SENATOR   Just like that.

JUDGE   The ease with which this country...

SENATOR   Let it. Let it! They want rid of us? We want rid of them. I like our odds! Justice? Whose justice? Ours? Theirs? You don't have it, judge. You don't have it! And even if you did, you wouldn't use it! You said so yourself. This country hangs by a thread. How'd justice go for us last time? How'd it solve our ills, huh? You don't have it! I'm staying! I'm staying, and I don't want you to be alarmed but I think we are going to have to take a look at that judicial practices thing again. These lifetime appointments... I don't know! People don't want justice, judge. They just don't! What we don't know can't hurt us. Ain't that the saying? All this begating... Well, it just ain't good for the soul, now is it? Violence needs violence! And what we don't know... Well, that's just the way of the world. Justice begats justice, judge. We want peace, we're just gonna have to renounce justice.

HE RISES TO EXIT.

SENATOR   I really am sorry about your boy. A tragedy. Truly. And after that... Well, I just don't know if I could carry on. You?

HE EXITS. LIGHTS DOWN ON THE JUDGE AS HE FADES AWAY.

END OF SCENE 2.

SCENE 3

AN OLD HOUSE ON THE OUTSKIRTS OF THE CITY. TWENTY YEARS BEFORE.

BEGAT

A SMALL GIRL – SENUR AS A CHILD – IS PLAYING IN FRONT OF HER FATHER, KIFUR, WHO IS ASLEEP IN AN ARM CHAIR.

OBVIOUSLY POOR, SHE IS PLAYING WITH A SOLITARY DOLL. SHE TWISTS THE DOLL AND AN ARM COMES OFF.

SHE TURNS TO HER FATHER.

YOUNG SENUR   Pappy.... Pappy...

KIFUR   What is it Senur?

YOUNG SENUR   I think Antolia is in trouble.

KIFUR   Is that right, darling?

YOUNG SENUR   Her arm's come off.

KIFUR   That is unfortunate.

YOUNG SENUR   She'll need fixing.

KIFUR   I expect she will.

UNSEEN TO KIFUR BUT OBVIOUS TO THE GIRL, THE JUDGE AND THE DOCTOR ENTER, BOTH WRAPPED IN LARGE OVERCOATS. THIS IS MANY YEARS AGO, AND BOTH MEN SEEM YOUNGER.

YOUNG SENUR   Pappy!

DOCTOR   Kifur.

KIFUR RISES. HE ALMOST SEEMS TO BE EXPECTING THE TWO MEN. THE JUDGE LOOKS AROUND DISAPPROVINGLY, STAMPING OFF THE COLD.

KIFUR   Hello doctor.

DOCTOR   How have you been, Kifur?

KIFUR   This and that.

JUDGE   We need to talk.

DOCTOR   This is Judge Alenvardos. He's... Well, we

have a few questions for you.

KIFUR   My daughter is here.

JUDGE   I'll look after her.

YOUNG SENUR   Pappy?

KIFUR   It's all right. Senur. Stay here.

THE DOCTOR AND KIFUR STEP AWAY TO TALK.

JUDGE   Hello.

YOUNG SENUR   Hello.

DOCTOR   We'll just go over here.

JUDGE   And who is this?

YOUNG SENUR   Antolia. Her arm's come off.

JUDGE   She looks like she's been in the wars.

YOUNG SENUR NODS.

JUDGE   (CONT.) Can I see her?

SHE HANDS THE DOLL OVER AND HE LOOKS FOR A WAY TO REATTACH THE ARM.

JUDGE   (CONT.) Do you know the story of toys? No? Well, I'll tell you! Toys are built with the biggest hearts. In fact, that's all they are. Hearts. You know what hearts are? Well, the problem with big hearts is that the bigger the heart is, the more precognisant they are. Do you know what that means? Precognisant? No? Well, you know when you can tell weather is coming, or... You are thinking about someone and then suddenly there they are, right in front of you! Yes? Well, it's like that. They can see the future. We only have little hearts, in proportion, so we can only see things a little way off. But toys, they are all heart. So every toy, from the moment they are made, they can see the future. Their future. All of it. They see when you buy them. They see when they come

BEGAT

home with you, what kind of home it is, and they see you growing. Changing. They see when they're important to you, and they see the day when you are just too big to play with them anymore. They even see the years of being stored away in boxes, or... Thrown away and... This is the thing with toys. With precognition. They can choose, whether they want to be with you! Whether they want to be with you or wait for another child to come into the store. By the look of Antolia she must love you very much.

DOCTOR   Judge?

THE JUDGE RISES AND JOINS THE TWO MEN. YOUNG SENUR STAYS WITH ANATOLIA.

THE DOCTOR NODS AS HE APPROACHES.

KIFUR   It was me.

JUDGE   Just like that?

KIFUR   I'm not sorry for it.

DOCTOR   Kifur...

JUDGE   You're not sorry?

KIFUR   It's their law!

JUDGE   Their...

DOCTOR   He says she was alive when he left her.

JUDGE   Their law! You... You raped a pregnant woman. Raped and hung.

DOCTOR   He's saying she wasn't dead.

KIFUR   I didn't know she was pregnant!

JUDGE   And that...

DOCTOR   Keep your voice down!

JUDGE   You've... You've seen what's happening? In the papers? Out there! The bloodshed!

KIFUR They killed my sister. Burnt her alive while she knelt in prayer.

DOCTOR They were...

JUDGE The... Damn you! That was...

KIFUR My sister was a righteous woman!

JUDGE It was a mistake. A mistake! There had been... As soon as they knew...

KIFUR It was not a mistake. They set fire to the...

JUDGE They set fire to the building because it was built on their lands! Ceremonial lands! They didn't know... your beliefs.

KIFUR Did they turn themselves in? Once they realised? Did they throw themselves on the mercy of your courts?

JUDGE They wouldn't have made it a day! They'd have been lynched!

KIFUR Their justice. Not mine. There's... There's not a... I'm ready to pay my price.

DOCTOR I think we can...

JUDGE It's genocide. Do you know that? Estimates are in the thousands. By the end of the month, there won't be any... The courts are flooded.

KIFUR They killed my sister. In prayer. I did not make their justice. I simply carried it out.

DOCTOR He's saying he didn't kill her.

KIFUR It was within the law.

SILENCE.

KIFUR I know what has to be done.

THE JUDGE PULLS A PISTOL OUT OF HIS COAT AND

BEGAT

LETS IT HANG AT HIS SIDE.

DOCTOR   Not here!

JUDGE   Where then? You'd take him into the capital? The court? Which court? It'd be on fire by morning. No. No one can know about this. I'm sorry. But no one can know! What happened… If we're going to have any chance of putting a lid on this thing… What happened… It's a myth. Fiction! You can't put a fire out with petrol. I'm sorry.

DOCTOR   I thought… I though justice done in secret couldn't be justice!

JUDGE   That's just something we tell people!

KIFUR   I don't regret what I did.

JUDGE   Then neither will I. Take the girl out front.

KIFUR   She has family. Across the border. With our people. They will look after her.

JUDGE   She'll be well taken care of, I promise. Take her out front.

DOCTOR   No! I…

KIFUR   Please. While my courage stands!

DOCTOR   Me. It should be me. My… Ilsa. It should be me.

KIFUR   Swear she'll be taken care of!

THE JUDGE HESITATES AND THEN HANDS THE DOCTOR THE GUN.

JUDGE   I promise

KIFUR TURNS AND KNEELS.

KIFUR   Quickly.

THE JUDGE TURNS AND SCOOPS YOUNG SENUR UP INTO HIS ARMS, HEADING FOR THE DOOR. THE

CHILD CRIES OUT FOR HER DOLL.

YOUNG SENUR Anatolia! Anatolia! No! Pappy!

THE JUDGE EXITS, HER ARMS AND FACE STREAMING OVER HIS SHOULDER INTO THE HOVEL.

DOCTOR   By the power invested...

KIFUR   No words. Just do it. If you're going to...

SILENCE. THE DOCTOR SEEMS HESITANT. THE GUN PRESSED AGAINST THE SIDE OF THE MAN'S TEMPLE.

KIFUR   Do you even know how...

THE GUN GOES OFF. KIFUR FALLS DEAD AS WE SMASH TO BLACKOUT.

CURTAINS.

THE END.

Thomas Alexander

Great

An Allegory in 4 Acts

CAST

CONSTANTINE - An old man.

REMUS - A middle aged man. A foreigner.

GETHIN - A young man/teenager. Son to CONSTANTINE.

AMERICA - A young woman/teenager. Wife to CONSTANTINE.

Thomas Alexander

ACT 1

Out on the far coast of nowhere, the wind lives caught and cut, rattling and moaning everything in its wake. Snowflakes on every breeze. Breathe in fog binders. Colder than cold.

A house, poor and sparse, wood and dust holding it up.

Two rough beds, no more than sacks, lie on either side of the room. Between them a table with two chairs, poor and well-worn, sit, sturdy and unmoving. A bottle and a cleaving knife are centre.

An old wood burning stove lies at the back of the room next to the door, a skillet on top used for cooking, a rough pot sitting central.

Two windows near the door show what appears to be a snow storm outside. Wind buffets the room and the entire theatre. It is cold. Snow seeps in through cracks in the door and windows, neither of which are closed properly, and swirls around the stage.

The room is timeless in that it could exist at any period in the 10th to 20th centuries, but there is no semblance of modern technology.

Time passes.

More time passes.

The door bursts open, whipping snow and wind across the stage. An old man, CONSTANTINE, struggles in through the storm. He is covered in a blanket to protect him, his clothes holed and threadbare.

In his gloved hand he holds a brace of rabbits caught in one of his snares.

The carcasses are frozen.

GREAT

He is having trouble closing the door against the snow. He leans his frail frame against it, but has to drop the rabbits before he has the leverage to finally get it closed.

Snow has crept deep into the house and the old man eyes it as he picks up the rabbits. There is not enough heat in the cabin to melt the snow and so, placing the rabbits on the table, he uses a brush to gather the drift before bending with difficulty to shovel it off the floor and into the stove.

He collects wood from the corner of the room and stacks it into the stove before going to a shelf, taking a book and tearing pages out. He delicately places them into the stove, careful so that the wind doesn't drag them away.

He digs a box of ageless matches out from inside his shirt. The wind tries to stop them lighting, but his practiced fingers get it at the first go, and he lights the papers and drops them into the stove.

A thin light waves from the stove and he warms his hands over it.

CONSTANTINE goes to the table, takes the stiff rabbits, and puts them next to the warmth.

There is a loud knock at the door.

The old man goes over to the window and looks out. He turns, shuffles to the door, and pulls it open as little as possible.

Two figures enter.

GETHIN, the old man's son, is as ragged and threadbare as he is. A virtual child, no more than a stick figure. With him is REMUS, old but not as old as CONSTANTINE, and considerably better dressed.

They both enter quickly, eager to escape the cold, but though REMUS is keen to shake the snow and cold from his clothes,

GETHIN remains obstinate, going quickly to a corner away from the other men and curling into it. Feral. Watching.

Together REMUS and CONSTANTINE manage to get the door closed again. CONSTANTINE moves wordlessly to the table and the bottle.

REMUS watches the old man, pity and revulsion in equal measures. He thinks about removing his gloves but realizing that the cold inside is almost as bad as outside he stops, casting instead a sad eye around the cabin.

This was the heart of his youth. A place of love and warmth. Now it is a decayed memory, much like CONSTANTINE.

REMUS   Can't keep doing this, Constantine.

CONSTANTINE wordlessly pulls out a chair for REMUS to sit on. He glares at GETHIN who holds his look.

REMUS sits.

CONSTANTINE takes two glasses and rubs them clean on his rags.

CONSTANTINE   Where?

REMUS   Timian's. Market.

CONSTANTINE scoops up fallen snow into the glasses and puts them on the table before pouring two drinks.

CONSTANTINE   He's an idiot.

REMUS watches him closely, shocked at what he's seeing. CONSTANTINE clinks glasses and sits. REMUS thinks about the statement, and puts the glass to one side before replying.

REMUS   Maybe. Yes. This can't go on, Constantine.

CONSTANTINE drinks. Sipping, savouring. The first in a long time. A special occasion.

GREAT

CONSTANTINE   He'll be hurt. You have my word.

REMUS thinks about this, then picks up his glass and downs it in one, disgusted by the comment as much as the drink.

CONSTANTINE is angered by his rush and doesn't offer to pour another.

REMUS   You remember Narvid? Of course you remember Narvid. He was… He was Narvid. (PAUSE) We expected you there, Constantine. (PAUSE) I can't keep vouching for the boy.

CONSTANTINE   Had to hunt.

REMUS looks around. Spies the frozen rabbits.

REMUS   He was at your wedding. (LONG PAUSE) You're not even going to ask what he stole?

CONSTANTINE looks at him, then uncorks the bottle and pours again. No snow. It sits untouched by REMUS.

REMUS   (CONT.) It was his horse, you remember? At the wedding? Eighteen hands at least. All I heard, outside the church, stamp, stamp. You remember?

CONSTANTINE stares out of the window, wishing the man to leave.

CONSTANTINE   Storm's coming.

REMUS turns to look.

REMUS   Doesn't matter. The boy… He loved you, you know? Narvid. Her too, but you. That horse… You remember? Lost it at the end. Nothing you can do about that, I think. We all lose it at the end. Mind and body, eh?

CONSTANTINE   You burn him?

REMUS nods and drinks.

REMUS   Ground's too hard.

CONSTANTINE nods.

REMUS   (CONT.) We thought you'd come.

CONSTANTINE   He'll work. The boy. For Timian.

REMUS   (AMUSED) Gethin? Work. Yes. Pocket's full, no doubt. Give him a week, he'll have the store. I'll… I'll pass it on to Timian. He'll be thrilled.

He drinks again, nearly choking. Then, without asking, refills.

CONSTANTINE notes the knife on the table.

REMUS   (CONT.) It doesn't matter. This is what I came to tell you. Narvid… You didn't even ask how he died.

CONSTANTINE   No.

REMUS   Found him four feet from his door. Four feet. Stooped on the step. Drifting…. Thawing… (PAUSE) Won't see a fire like that in some time.

CONSTANTINE   Say it.

REMUS looks at him and thinks. He is not in a hurry.

REMUS   I caught this fish, before the storm hit. The lake… (BEAT) When was the last time you ate fish, Constantine? What do you… There's a hole. On the far side, no one else knows about it. Only me. It's where – do you remember – it's where we used to dive. In the summers. Same place. It's shaded and the ice doesn't get too thick and you can hole it with your boot if you know it well enough. And, well, I did. Hole it. And… It was a good day, you remember? Good sun on your neck. Not looking to catch anything, just… fishing. Not looking to catch anything. And… Third hour, nothing but the sun and the branches, you know what I mean? Beautiful. And I feel it. You know? A pull. Nothing big, just the gentlest of pulls, like he's slowly leaning against

GREAT

it, you know what I mean? So… I ease, nothing much. Ease. And snap! Just like that! Now, I'm running the line, everything I've got to keep the reel in my hand, you know what I mean? Twenty, thirty! And I'm thinking, how much line do I have, and snap! My arms! Nearly out their sockets! So, I'm hauling. This is not a good line. I'm not looking to catch anything, you understand? But I'm hauling all the same. And I can feel it, you know? The sun on my neck. Hours are passing. Reel. Release. But now all I'm thinking about is how I don't want to lose the rod, you know? Can't reach for my knife! I take a hand off the rod, it's gone. Far too big for the line. So, no choice. Reel and release. Who gets tired first, you know? And… I'm calling. To the fish, I'm calling! Talking to him. Why you want my rod? You think this is going to do you any good? Rod like this one hanging out your mouth? How you going to eat with a rod like this behind you? Who'll want you? And I can feel it, you know? Going down on my neck. The sun. Fingers… like ice! But what can I do? I've got a home, I tell him. A woman is waiting for me! I promise everything. Let him go. Everything. And I can see them, you know, the shadows, getting the light. (RESIGNED) Anyway. (BANGING THE TABLE) Boom! He hits the ice, right beneath my feet! And I can feel him. The size on him! Turned on me! Boom, right under me! All I can do to hang on. And the hole. It's closing. I can see it. Closing around the line. Can he even take the rod? And I guess he's thinking the same thing because this time, this time, he comes for me through the hole! Now, it's dark. Shadows only and… Is it his nose, his head? I can't tell, but I've got him. Tight. Two feet of line maximum! Right in the palm of my hand, and I'm thinking, who cares about the cold! Who cares about dinner! This! This is dinner! Twenty dinners! War! You know what I mean? I've got him. Water, ice – red!

He sits back. Resigned.

REMUS (CONT.) Can't get the hole big enough. Can't do it! Touched it. Right there. Twenty… Can't do it. (BEAT) Watched the line sink right into the ice. Rod with it. (PAUSE) Couldn't even free him.

He drinks and pours again, not caring about the glass any more. CONSTANTINE watches again, angry.

CONSTANTINE You're leaving.

REMUS (BITTER AT THE DRINK) We're leaving. The Village. All of us. (PAUSE) Two days. Three, if the weather holds up. This is no place for a man, Constantine. No matter the history.

CONSTANTINE rises. He heads to the stove, glaring at GETHIN.

A sense of violence pervades the room.

Silence.

CONSTANTINE Stay for rabbit.

REMUS No. (PAUSE) It's decided. Three days at the latest, Constantine.

Pause.

CONSTANTINE Storms won't last.

Pause.

REMUS It's decided.

Pause.

CONSTANTINE (ENDING THE CONVERSATION) Tell Timian he'll be hurt.

REMUS And that's that?

Pause.

CONSTANTINE Yes.

GREAT

REMUS drinks again, choking. He looks set to leave but suddenly decided against it and pours himself another.

REMUS   No. No. Come. Sit down, Constantine. Sit down! I'll pay you for another bottle. Sit down!

CONSTANTINE sits, the knife close to him on the table. It is a gesture not unnoticed by REMUS, but his mind is set.

REMUS   (CONT.) There's no lightning here! You know that. Not anymore. When we were young... (PAUSE) We're going across the lake. All of us. Far ridge. There has to be... (PAUSE) The boy doesn't deserve this.

CONSTANTINE   You pay for the whole bottle.

Silence. GETHIN stirs. REMUS pours.

REMUS   There is this man. He comes into the camp from time to time. Not from here. He brings goods, things to sell. Lightning. He comes, maybe a month ago. A little more. He brings with him this... box. A lightening box, he says. So, I say to him. What is that to me? This is not a large box, maybe the size of your head. Little bigger. So, he says to me, he says, this box is the future. I swear! This box is the future! Just like that. He tells me everyone can get this box. Everyone! Where he comes from this is normal. So obviously I believe none of it. Okay, I say, the future. Sure. But he is buying the bottle so I listen. This box, he says, this box everybody has. And this box... This is all you need, yes? Simple as that. With this box you can... Snow does not come in the door like that! Snow inside, this is a thing of the past. Rabbits... Whatever you want! So I say, sure, sure! Completely. And then he shows me! So simple! So... Like nothing you have ever seen. Just a box! And standing there, like that! He says to me, stand up, so... Like that. And he opens the box. And there, there, right there! Every detail! A picture of me. Like that! No time, no…. (HE FUMBLES FOR THE WORD) sulphur… Phosphorous. No phosphorous! Nothing. Like that. Just there! He takes a picture of me. I have it in my house. And he tells me, we can bring this here! To the camp. You know. OK, so what for, I say. And he laughs at me. Laughs! What for? Why would you live without it? How long have we known each other, Constantine? How long, eh? A long time! I can tell you the pegs in this table. You remember? Steady as a rock I held it. You, hammering away while she was cooking? Out there. In the spring. That door! There isn't a thing in this house doesn't have my fingerprints on it. Look at you now, yes. Look how you are living. (RESIGNED) I would ask you to come with us but… But the boy? Yes. Think about the boy? About Gethin. Without the Village? What have you got? The forests to hunt in. (GESTURING TO THE RABBITS) The odd set to still dig up? Without the camp, how long do you think you can survive up here, eh? With nothing. No money? Can't trap bottles!

CONSTANTINE   (MENACINGLY) He stays. You go!

REMUS studies him, then shrugs.

REMUS   Your world. (HE THINKS ABOUT LEAVING) What do you want me to tell Timian?

CONSTANTINE   Tell him what you like.

REMUS   He will want compensation. I promised I'd talk to you.

CONSTANTINE   What does he want?

REMUS   He's Timian. An apology from you would not go amiss but… Well, high horses will fly before that happens. (BEAT) I'll take one of the rabbits.

He rises, heading for the rabbits. CONSTANTINE grabs his

GREAT

arm. REMUS pauses.

CONSTANTINE   The bottle!

REMUS thinks about challenging him, then acquiesces and reaches into a pocket. He thumbs through a few coins and deposits the minor ones on the table. CONSTANTINE releases his arm.

REMUS goes to the rabbits and selects one, cutting the cord that binds it to the others.

REMUS   She would have hated to see you like this, Constantine. The man you've become? Independence... We understand independence but this... Think about it. He is barely more than an urchin now. Where would he be without the Village! Think about it, okay?

CONSTANTINE moves over to the door, ready to open it. REMUS wraps himself in preparation for the cold.

REMUS   (CONT.) Think about it.

CONSTANTINE opens the door just enough for REMUS to squeeze through, which he does. CONSTANTINE struggles to close the door again.

GETHIN stays where he is.

The door closed, CONSTANTINE goes to the rabbits. He takes one over to the table and, grabbing the knife from where he'd left it on the table, he beheads it and begins to skin it.

Slowly, cautiously, GETHIN rises and goes over to the stove. He goes unwatched by CONSTANTINE as he picks up the snow that has seeped in and puts it into the fire.

He relaxes slightly and makes his way back across the room towards his bed.

As he passes CONSTANTINE lashes out, hitting the boy in the face and sending him to the ground. The sudden casualness of the action is shocking but the old man never looks at the fallen boy who has blood running from his nose.

The boy, inert on the floor, waits for further reprisals but the old man continues with the skinning.

Slowly, cautiously, the boy rises. From within his ragged clothes he pulls some bread he has stolen.

Gingerly, as if approaching a wild animal, he holds out the bread and puts it on the table, all the time expecting another hit.

A potato comes the same way, then a carrot. He waits for his father's approval.

With the rabbit skinned, CONSTANTINE looks at the money on the table, then at the produce. He upends the knife and drives it deep into the table.

FADE TO BLACK.

END OF ACT 1.

GREAT

ACT 2

It is night time in the cabin.

Outside the snow storm has stopped, but the howl of the wind continues to shake the room.

A fresh full moon shines in through the window. A thick candle is the only other light. The room is filled with ominous shadows and dark corners.

On the stove is a pot containing rabbit stew.

CONSTANTINE, drunk, is sitting on his bed in a state of mild undress. A bottle is clutched carelessly in his hand.

At his feet GETHIN is trying to get his boots off.

The old man is singing, sadly, almost internally.

CONSTANTINE   Five hundred sons my hand ran through / Five hundred hands from me to you / Five hundred widows at the grave / Five hundred times this soul I gave. / Five hundred sons my hand did end / Five hundred times to make amends / Five hundred men that I saw die / The last of the five hundred: I!

His father's feet free, GETHIN moves to take the bottle. Again the old man swings out catching the boy violently, but this one is expected and the boy barely pauses as he moves to aid the old man back onto his bed.

Immediately the old man breaks into a rhythmic snore.

GETHIN turns to the table and deposits the candle, blowing it out.

The knife is still stuck in the table and, checking that the old man cannot see him, he takes it before he makes his way to his own bed in the opposite corner.

The two men are drowned in shadows. Only the wind and

moonlight remain.

The old man chokes and wakes.

Pause.

GETHIN: Who was that brought me to the house?

CONSTANTINE: Sleep.

GETHIN: Who was that brought me here.

CONSTANTINE: No one. No one. None of them!

GETHIN: He knew ma?

CONSTANTINE: None of them!

GETHIN: You knew him

CONSTANTINE: Yes

GETHIN: I knew him?

CONSTANTINE: Many times. He used to come here.

GETHIN: I don't know that.

CONSTANTINE: Always caught you.

GETHIN: I don't know that. (PAUSE) How old was I?

CONSTANTINE: Why?

GETHIN: I don't remember him.

Silence.

CONSTANTINE: Tell me. (SILENCE) Tell me!

Outside a wolf howls. Another answers.

GETHIN: Close.

CONSTANTINE: Tell me.

GETHIN: (RECITING) They came from the east.

CONSTANTINE: Yes.

GREAT

GETHIN Course of them.

CONSTANTINE Yes.

A wolf howls.

GETHIN She was the most beautiful creature he had seen, this land or another.

CONSTANTINE Eyes like…

GETHIN Eyes like sapphire. She wore a white dress and hair in red. Steepled like a beggars' hands.

A wolf howls. CONSTANTINE answers with one of his own.

GETHIN (CONT.) They were married under the tree – the fire tree – down at the end of the camp. Only it wasn't the fire tree then. It was just a tree. The fire tree would come later.

CONSTANTINE She wore green!

GETHIN Yes.

CONSTANTINE And her hands were so cold!

GETHIN You buried yourselves under the water, by the fire tree, in the river, the bear high above you. Great bear! Cupped in moonlight.

A wolf starts to howl. CONSTANTINE joins it in chorus. GETHIN waits for them to finish before going on.

GETHIN (CONT.) You buried yourselves for the whole Village to watch, and when you rose, under the bear, the whole Village carried you back to the tavern.

CONSTANTINE Green.

GETHIN And then they came.

CONSTANTINE Yes.

GETHIN Not that night. Not the night after. The great bear moved on. Orion's belt measured the pair of you. (PAUSE) And you (BEAT) gloried in each other. Gorged each other. Like wild animals mount, you mounted. (BEAT) And everyone cheered.

CONSTANTINE   Yes.

GETHIN   And then they came. Kind like. Inside the camp. Right under your very own doorstep.

CONSTANTINE   Right there.

GETHIN   And they devoured the Village. Monsters of men! Blood handed from the bottomless slain. They tore at the very shred of us. Of all of us! Of children!

Another howl from outside. This time there is no response.

GETHIN   (CONT.) Cousin against cousin. End against end. They came over the ridge and saw the camp and the lake beyond it, and waded into us.

Pause.

GETHIN   (CONT.) No man could stand against them. Some… fled. Others fell. They cut and they chewed and they gave no edge for hope. And so they called him. They called you. And you were deep in love. Buried. Warm. And they dug you up with their calling. Sought you out. The Village, red with blood, light with fire. They called to you and you stretched and you answered, as you always answered, as you had always answered. And so you bathed. And you spent hammer on metal. And you clothed yourself for war. (BEAT) And you left her.

CONSTANTINE   Yes.

GETHIN   With new life inside her, you left her. (PAUSE) And the plain was burning. High as a horse it was burning but you cut through it. Cut through it to crash into the camp. What you saw there! The whispers of men!

GREAT

Old enemies licking like dogs the feet that had down trod them. Friends turned black with blood, shading themselves with the clothes of their conquerors. And so you cut them! You! Under Orion's belt you cut them! Best and the worst. Hundreds deep! And you laid them at your feet, gripping their flesh with your toes until the ground they fought on was no more than entrails! Fled or fallen. Fled or fallen they leave. The men of the east exorcised from the Village. How long have you gloried in the blood of your enemies? How long have you carried the weight of the camp? Long enough for life to come beyond the ridge. Long enough for baby's cries to rattle these walls. (SOTTO, HIS OWN ADDITION) Long enough for these lungs.

A long wolf howl, far away. CONSTANTINE is silent. Asleep once more.

Pause.

Almost unseen in the dark, moving slowly to avoid any noise, GETHIN has moved himself into a seated position on the edge of the bed.

In his hand he holds the knife.

GETHIN   (CONT.) She was gone. When you returned. Like the air gone. The baby lying on the bed where he had her. Warm in her blood.

The old man is asleep. The boy listening for his breathing hears a snore just before a wolf howls.

GETHIN rises, tucking the knife out of sight of the moonlight. The wind, rising, rattles the door and the boy uses it to mask his movements as he tiptoes across to the sleeping old man, knife in hand, purpose clear.

He is almost on him when the wind blows the door open, flooding the room with moonlight.

The boy falls on the old man, trying to force the knife to his throat, but the old man has woken and is rising.

He clenches the boy's arm as it pushes for his throat.

The boy puts his weight behind it but it's not enough. The old man twists the arm down and head-butts the boy.

The knife spins away onto the floor and the boy flails backwards, skidding behind the lost knife.

GETHIN (CONT.) No!

But the old man is on him, his hands at his throat.

A wolf howls, close now. Wind whips the stage.

The old man looks at the open, flapping door. He hits the boy brutally and drags him, half unconscious, to the threshold.

The boy starts to stir just in time to find himself thrown out into the snow.

He lets out a cry and rising struggles for the closing door, leaning his weight against it.

GETHIN (CONT.) No! Papa, no!

But the old man's anger is enough to conquer his son and the wind.

As it closes, a wolf howls.

Silence.

The old man leans against the door.

Then starts the banging. Loud crashes rock the door and the old man, who starts to fear the entire wall might fall.

GETHIN (CONT., LOUDLY OFF) Papa! Papa! Please! Papa!

Amidst the calls and bangs, the wolves start again, numerous voices loud, near and far. A cacophony drowning out even the pounding on the door.

GREAT

GETHIN (CONT., LOUDLY OFF) Papa, papa! Open the door! Papa! Please! (ETC.)

CONSTANTINE (SCREAMING) Tell it!

GETHIN (LOUDLY OFF) Papa! (ETC.)

CONSTANTINE covers his ears against the noise

CONSTANTINE Tell it!

GETHIN (LOUDLY OFF) Papa! Please! Please!

The howls of the wolves, the banging on the door, the screams of his son, all reach a crescendo, the old man nearly doubled over at the noise.

CONSTANTINE (SCREAMING) Teeeeeellllllll iiiiiiiittttt!

Silence.

No wolves. No banging. No cries.

Even the wind has dissipated.

The old man unfurls. He rises slowly, his back to the door, listening for the sound of anything.

Suddenly, scared, he turns and opens the door.

GETHIN is lying in the snow behind the door. Further out we see the green eyes of a pack of wolves, mere feet away.

CONSTANTINE (CONT.) Away with you! Away!

He grabs the prone boy and drags him back into the cabin, throwing him onto the floor before returning to the doorway.

Stretching out against the door lintels, he rages into the night.

CONSTANTINE (CONT.) Away with you! You hear me! All of you!

The wind and wolves, as if answering, let out a cry. The old man is buffeted as he stands in the doorway, the first flakes of a new snow storm drifting in through the opening, catching in his hair and beard.

CONSTANTINE   (CONT.) I don't need you! You hear me! You hear me! Go! You want to go, go! I don't need you! You think I need you! I don't need any of you! Any of you! He's mine! Do you hear me? Mine! My blood! You want him? You want him? He's mine and I will do whatever with him! Whatever I want!

The wolves withdraw.

CONSTANTINE   (CONT.) Come at me! Come at me, if you dare! I will end you! All of you! Come at me!

Only the wind buffets him now. Only the snow.

CONSTANTINE   (CONT.) He's mine, do you hear me? Mine! My blood! You want to go, go! All of you! But he! Is! Mine!

GETHIN is rising.

GETHIN   Papa!

CONSTANTINE   (OBLIVIOUS) Come at me if you're coming! I dare you! Come on! Come at me! What are you waiting for?

GETHIN goes to him and tries to pull him back into the house.

GETHIN	Papa! Please! Papa.
CONSTANTINE	Where are you, eh? Where are you?
GETHIN	Papa! Stop it! Please!
CONSTANTINE	Mine! You hear me!
GETHIN	Papa!
CONSTANTINE	Get off me!
GETHIN	Come back in!

GREAT

CONSTANTINE   Get off me!

But the old man is acquiescing, allowing the boy to drag him back inside and together they start to close the door.

GETHIN   Papa…

CONSTANTINE   Push! God damn you!

They push the door shut, the snow picking up.

They stand there, wheezing. The old man looks at his son, both of them shivering in the cold.

He calmly, almost affectionately, delivers a backhand blow that sends the boy to the floor once more before proceeding to the table and the bottle.

CONSTANTINE   Tell it!

GETHIN remains silent. The old man drinks.

CONSTANTINE   (CONT., SOFTLY) Tell it, damn you.

GETHIN   (WEARY) They came from the east.

This time the old man's responses are in contrast. Strong. Full of pride.

CONSTANTINE   Yes.

GETHIN   Courses of them.

CONSTANTINE   Yes! (HE DRINKS, THEN FONDLY) Tell it!

GETHIN   She was the most beautiful creature he had seen, this land or another. Eyes like sapphire. She wore a white dress and hair in red. Steepled like a beggar's hands. They were married under the tree – the fire tree – down at the end of the camp. Only it wasn't the fire tree then. It was just a tree. The fire tree would come later. You buried yourselves under the water, by the fire tree, in the river, the bear high above you. Cupped in moonlight. You buried yourselves, for the whole camp to watch, and when you rose, the whole camp carried you back to the tavern.

As the story unfolds the boy curls himself into a ball from the cold and the old man drinks.

Clouds scour the moon casting the room into fits of blackness, increasing in darkness with every pass until finally the story is being told in complete obscurity.

GETHIN   And then they came.

END OF ACT 2.

ACT 3

Daytime.

Inside the house GETHIN is alone.

Outside the storm has abated.

He is struggling with the pot from the stove. Carrying it over to the table he removes the lid and, rolling up a sleeve, slides his hand into the broth, searching along the bottom.

He finds what he's looking for and pulls out a piece of bone. He picks the meat off, dropping it back into the stew, and then carefully sucks the bone dry before placing it on the table.

He does this several more times, fishing and finding as many bones as he can, never interested in the meat.

Through it all he keeps watch on the door.

GREAT

Satisfied that there are no more bones to be found he pulls down his sleeve without wiping his arm, replaces the lid, and returns the pan to its place on the stove.

He scampers across to his bed and pulls out a box from a hidden position behind his mattress.

Returning to the table he opens the box and pulls out a knotted handkerchief. He opens it to reveal more bones of all sizes and a collection of odd string. Comparing the new bones to them he adds them to the collection before reaching into the box once more and returning with three or four sculptures.

He is making bone monsters. Delicate, incredibly crafted statues made out of bone and string, they stand on the table a mixture of craftsmanship, ingenuity and horror. They are beautiful and twisted: a cat's jaw on a mouse's spine, frog's legs with a human finger.

Creatively speaking, they are works of genius.

Before we do, he hears footsteps approaching and moves to put away the statues.

In his eagerness he knocks one off the table and, squealing in horror, is in the process of picking up the pieces when REMUS enters.

REMUS   Constantine!

He sees the boy and pauses.

REMUS   (CONT.) Constantine?

GETHIN   Out!

REMUS sees the sculptures and heads for them. GETHIN moves to block him, pawing at the man as he tries to approach.

REMUS   What've you got here?

GETHIN   No!

REMUS shrugs him off, his hand on the arm GETHIN had

in the soup.

REMUS Get off! (LOOKING AT HIS HAND) God, you're… filthy animal!

GETHIN backs off as if stung.

REMUS picks up one of the statues

REMUS (CONT.) What have we here?

GETHIN Mine!

REMUS (ANGERED) I'm not taking them. I'm just having a… You made these, did you? On your own? There's… Who taught you to do this, boy?

GETHIN They're mine!

REMUS There's… There's craftsmen…

REMUS spies something in the box and retrieves it. GETHIN tries to snatch it before he does but REMUS is too quick.

It is a photo. Old. Faded.

REMUS Well, well! God, she was something! Look at her! A man could stand exile with something like that… Does he tell you about her, boy? Does he tell you what she was like?

GETHIN Green.

REMUS He was something to be feared in those days!

GETHIN Mine!

REMUS Nothing is ours boy. Best learn that.

The door opens revealing CONSTANTINE who enters carrying his bride.

Though not noticeably younger, he is clearly more vital, brimming with power despite his age.

AMERICA is young, far too young and beautiful for a man

GREAT

like him.

She is laughing.

CONSTANTINE   Woopsie! Here we go… One, two…

She giggles.

On three the old man crosses the threshold. The hovel is suddenly bathed in warm sunlight. Cobwebs magically disappearing. Though still a hovel it is a warm, magical one.

The bride looks around and likes what she sees.

At the front of the stage GETHIN and REMUS disappear into the shadow of the table.

AMERICA   Oh, it's…

He drops her down, still full of vigour.

CONSTANTINE   Yes, not much, but home. Home! Let me look at you.

AMERICA   (PULLING AWAY PLAYFULLY) No, I want to see it! (BEAT) Home!

CONSTANTINE   If you'll have me.

AMERICA starts to tour the room.

AMERICA   This… This is our bed? Our bed.

CONSTANTINE   Home.

AMERICA   Our stove?

CONSTANTINE   Something else to heat us!

AMERICA   (BEAT) Our table.

CONSTANTINE   Where I'll have you as well!

AMERICA   (TEASING) Aren't you too old for that?

CONSTANTINE   Meat on my bones.

AMERICA   You'll need a nap soon.

CONSTANTINE   I'll be running you through before that!

AMERICA   Have to catch me first!

They start to chase, AMERICA putting objects between them.

AMERICA   (CONT.) Catch me!

She puts a chair in front of him and he flicks it away with a roar, catching her arm and pulling her into him.

They kiss.

AMERICA   (CONT.) You won't miss it?

CONSTANTINE   What's mine to miss?

AMERICA   Castles, lands…

CONSTANTINE   Exploring to be done right here!

She squirms away in delight.

AMERICA   And if they come?

CONSTANTINE   I'll kill them!

AMERICA   And if they fight?

CONSTANTINE   Cut their throats! (HE GRABS HER) Take more than the lands to keep me from you.

Belieing his age he lifts her onto the table and the two fall about each other.

The old man is annoyed. No matter the passion, something is wrong. He fumbles at her, getting increasingly frustrated.

CONSTANTINE   (CONT.) Damn it!

Beneath the table GETHIN covers his ears but REMUS stands and moves around the room watching them. When he gets near the door, he coughs and the couple turn around.

AMERICA   Remus!

CONSTANTINE   (ANGERED) Bald faced bastard!

GREAT

AMERICA No!

AMERICA stills him, breaks free.

AMERICA (CONT.) None of that! You hear me? Remus is a friend. Your friend!

She hugs REMUS.

The two men eye each other.

AMERICA (CONT.) Remus! It's good to see you again!

REMUS (TO CONSTANTINE) So, you've returned?

CONSTANTINE I have!

REMUS No more lands for you?

AMERICA Stop it! You are brothers! Once upon a time. And now!

CONSTANTINE I'm hungry.

AMERICA How are you Remus? Bronzed, it would seem.

REMUS The Village is eager for you to join them, Constantine. We could use your arm, and your... wisdom.

CONSTANTINE Fuck the Village! And fuck you, brother. Everything I need is here!

REMUS No one is alone.

CONSTANTINE Alone? Is that right? Do I look alone? (To AMERICA) Get us bread!

The bride does as she is told.

REMUS I'm sorry you feel like that, Constantine.

CONSTANTINE What is it about men, hmm? Fuck

us once and you think you can fuck us again. Is that it? I don't need the Village and it doesn't need me. Understand that? Can you get that into your thick skull? Hmm? Far as I'm concerned, you can all burn!

REMUS   Is that what it taught you?

CONSTANTINE   Hmm? What was that?

REMUS   Is that what it taught you? Over the lake?

CONSTANTINE   Take care with your tone!

REMUS   No, I don't think I will!

AMERICA   Stop it! Both of you! Husband… Remus, you are… always welcome here. Always! This was your home!

CONSTANTINE   Like fuck it was!

AMERICA   Husband! (TO REMUS) You are always welcome here. (TO HER HUSBAND) There's no water. (HE DOESN'T HEAR) Husband? Water!

CONSTANTINE   What's that?

AMERICA   There's no water. Not here.

CONSTANTINE   So?

AMERICA   You might get some… for our guest. Unless you want him to drink all the wine?

CONSTANTINE   Fucker's staying that long?

AMERICA   Enough! Water! Please.

CONSTANTINE   (GLARING AT REMUS) Fine!

They watch him exit. Silence as REMUS looks around the cabin, AMERICA stands with her back against the table watching her husband depart down the hill for the water.

REMUS picks up a metal poker.

GREAT

AMERICA Do you miss it?
REMUS Hmm?
AMERICA I would, I think. Had I grown up here.
REMUS As many bad memories as good.
AMERICA Was he rough with you? At the end.
REMUS All men are rough. It's in our nature.
AMERICA (FLIRTING) He is with me.

REMUS stops, looks at her.

AMERICA (CONT.) You are right about him.
REMUS What am I right about him?
AMERICA What you're thinking.
REMUS What am I thinking?
AMERICA How long over the lake was he. How many children.
REMUS I wouldn't know.
AMERICA But you're thinking it.
REMUS I think many things.
AMERICA I'm glad to hear it!

Silence

AMERICA (CONT.) The well pum...
REMUS When I lived here... When I was young with him... I picked up this before. It's not this one, but he taught me how to make it. Taught me how to make it, bending metal over and over in a furnace. Over and over, and then he'd hit me with it. Not a man to cross.

He is nearer her now.

AMERICA The well pump is broken.

They stare at each other.

REMUS America...

AMERICA Hush!

Swiftly REMUS reaches out and pulls back her hair, his mouth inches from hers. She doesn't resist.

AMERICA (CONT.) It's alright.

He mounts her quickly, as much in anger as passion. She pulls him into her.

REMUS Tell me you love me!

Silence.

REMUS (CONT.) Tell me!

But there is no response. And she buries his mouth in hers to silence him.

Their coupling is quick and powerful. As he finishes she pulls him in deeply.

Sated he leans into her and she strokes his hair.

AMERICA (AS IF TO A CHILD) There. Hush... It's over now... Hush. Hush.

Hearing this he pulls away, covering himself as he does.

AMERICA (CONT.) You have names for me?

REMUS Come with me!

AMERICA (LAUGHING) Do you imagine? No. You are beautiful Remus. He will be a fantastic boy!

REMUS I don't understand you.

AMERICA Go out the back way now. Pumps don't stay broken.

REMUS Come with me.

AMERICA They have bluebird where I come

GREAT

from. Not like here. Blue. Birds. With actual blue feathers and… They look so pretty, in the sky, flying above you. Out of reach. But these birds. You know, you can take the feathers of a bird, any bird, and make the best poisons in the world. All of them. Grind down the feathers, dry the powder. Why is that, you think? That they are so poisonous to men? But these blue birds. Delicious! You bake them, roast some chestnuts in their stomachs. Some rosemary…. You have to pluck them carefully of course. Nothing is more poisonous than their feathers, but delicious. Look after yourself, Remus. Look after him if you live.

He looks at her.

AMERICA (CONT.) Now. Go!

REMUS crosses past her to an unseen exit downstage.

As he passes she reaches out and digs her nails into his arm, marking him.

AMERICA (CONT.) That is to remember me by!

She scratches deep into his arm. He twists away in pain and stares at her in bewilderment.

AMERICA (CONT.) Now go!

REMUS returns to his position next to GETHIN.

AMERICA sits, quietly. Sad but with a sense of accomplishment.

Outside her husband calls.

CONSTANTINE (OFF) Wife!

She looks up. Goes to the door.

CONSTANTINE (CONT., OFF) Wife.

She pauses, then moves out after him.

AMERICA What are we mewling now, husband?

Thomas Alexander

Exit AMERICA.

Lights up on REMUS and GETHIN.

The cabin has returned to its state of disrepair, the memories of the past extinguished.

REMUS is holding one of the bone monsters up to the light. GETHIN looks at him as if he was holding his soul.

REMUS   Read, can you?

The boy shakes his head.

REMUS   (CONT.) Numbers?

Another shake.

REMUS   (CONT.) Rag of a boy, aren't you? What are these things?

GETHIN gently takes the sculpture back.

GETHIN   They live beyond the lake.

REMUS   That right?

The boy starts taking the animals one by one from the box and shows them to the fascinated and repulsed REMUS.

GETHIN   Over the lake they taxes them. Words. You speak and you get taxed. They got... This one... He is the great speaker, right. An'... And he uses lots of words and so they taxes him. They taxes him so he can't use the word no more. An' the words... The words, they get angry at this cos taxes are bad, aren't they. So they get angry at this and they don't come no more, the words, and this one... This one... He's got to speak, right. For the Village... He's got to speak but the words don't come no more because they be taxed and don't like it. (PAUSE) That's why they don't come no more. Across the lake. Words.

Pause.

GREAT

REMUS   Had a horse like you. Once. Good legs. Strong. Mind like a fig. Stood hands above the rest of them! Every bone in his body muscled perfectly. Could I train it? I could not! Thousand times round the harness and every time like the first. (PAUSE) Still wouldn't be the first time.

Enter CONSTANTINE.

This time when CONSTANTINE enters the snow whips the room. There is no sunlight to greet him.

All three cower from the wind and drive, GETHIN hunching quickly over his statues, focused on getting them back into the box before CONSTANTINE notices.

CONSTANTINE struggles with the door, using all his efforts to close it once more behind the sudden snow storm.

The storm is getting worse.

The door secured, he shakes snow from his mane and sees REMUS at the table.

He pauses. In his hand a pail of iced water is set down, and he adjusts his knife as he speaks.

CONSTANTINE   Again?

REMUS   I thought to give you one last chance. (HE BRUSHES SNOW FROM HIS HAIR) You'll be buried soon.

CONSTANTINE takes the pail to the stove and then moves across to the table.

He pulls a root vegetable from his cloak. It is frozen but he begins hacking at it with his knife as he watches his old adversary in love.

Carefully REMUS sits down near him. GETHIN scuttles to hide his box. The two glance at him.

CONSTANTINE   Find what you want?

REMUS   Timian wants him. For the shop. In fact he… What he says… He owns him, for the stealing.

CONSTANTINE begins to gnaw on the strips of vegetable.

CONSTANTINE   Been paid.

REMUS   One rabbit is not… It appears to be more than that, the theft. Timian… He does not want people involved. Your good name…. He says he wants to take the boy. With him. Across the lake. He will train him, give him purpose. This he promises. Fit punishment, I think. You can come too.

CONSTANTINE   Boy stays.

Silence.

REMUS   I ever tell you about the boat, Constantine?

CONSTANTINE   More stories, Remus?

Suddenly alive, REMUS produces a flask from inside his coat.

REMUS   Meh, the snow is too strong to go out. Look, for us! One last drink between friends? Old friends, okay? One last story.

The old man watches him as he looks for cups.

REMUS   The Village is nearly packed, Constantine. Mid-morning, tomorrow. Day after, depending on the storms. Soon we will be gone, eh? Out of your hair? Unless you change your mind..? No, I can see not. Still one last drink. One last story for old friends.

He puts three cups on the table. Instantly CONSTANTINE picks one up and throws it across the room at GETHIN who ducks out of its way.

REMUS is incensed and reaches inside his clothes, presumably for a weapon. CONSTANTINE glares at him.

GREAT

CONSTANTINE   Not for him!

REMUS thinks, then shrugs. His earlier mask of effusion returning. He pours.

REMUS   Fine, fine. You treat him too hard, Constantine. Always have. Boy is wild in all but name. But, your son. Your son. I told Timian as much. You cannot make him give up his son, I told him. Yes, he steals. Yes, he owes you, but the other side of the lake..? This is too much. I told him this!

CONSTANTINE   The boat?

REMUS   (CONFUSED) Sorry?

CONSTANTINE   You were telling me about the boat?

REMUS   Oh. Yes. Well… I cannot tell you about the boat! You know all about the boat! Who but you, eh? No. Still. This time… I have not taken the boat like you have, Constantine. All that back and fore, back and fore! Days were you lived on the boat, did you not? No, I have… Once or twice, no more. So, for me, it is still a big adventure, yes? When we sail, when the Village crosses, big adventure! But, that is now. This is then. Much then. I… You had just returned. A year, tops, and I thought of you. I did! I thought, Constantine crossed the lake. Why not I? Yes! So I crossed. You know what this is like.

He pauses. Drinks.

REMUS   (CONT.) You remember before the lightning? You remember that? How the world changes, eh. How were we so wrong? I ask you that. Seriously. For so long, so wrong. How can that be? Expansion, yes? This is all we talked about. Those nights by the fire, when we built this place. This table, eh? Expansion! The Village! Where to next, that's what we used to ask ourselves. So simple. So simple!

Where to next. We were... whirlwinds! Whirlwinds! Now here, now here!

He tops the old man's drink.

REMUS (CONT.) Now where are we? Hmm? We reached everything. Everything! And... Yes, when we got there, but... Expansion. That was what we talked about. Expansion. Now? Who wants expansion anymore? Who wants all the bother? Give us lightning! This is what we ask. Give us lightning! Small worlds full of lightning. When you came back... When you brought her here... You were my idol! You know that? Expansion! Then you came back.

He drinks.

CONSTANTINE The boat.

REMUS Right. Yes. So, well, you came back and I thought, why not! So I took the boat. And then, right there... I saw it, Constantine. I saw it! Lights in the darkness, that's all we are! Pinpricks of lights! I stood there, on the deck, and I'm looking out at... nothing. Nothing! No stars, no sea, nothing! Blackness and then I see it. This light. Tiny, ahead of me. And I hold up my thumb, just so, and I hold it, and the light goes. (HE MOVES HIS THUMB) Light, no light. Light, no light. Hours I do this. Hours. Light, no light. And at times, I think the light is bigger. Sometimes it fits around my thumb and then it's nothing again, banished by a digit. Banished. But, little by little, it grows. A ship. Naturally. Moving towards and away at the same time. Towards and away. Saddest thing I've ever seen.

CONSTANTINE takes the flask and empties the contents into his cup.

REMUS We were... It was the only way we could be proud. The only way... We used to be about the

GREAT

expansion of the Village. Now we are only about the expansion of ourselves.

CONSTANTINE downs the rest of his drink and rises, done.

REMUS (CONT.) You have to let him go, Constantine.

CONSTANTINE swings out an arm and catches REMUS, sending him back off his chair.

REMUS is unprepared for the attack and spins ungainly onto the floor, scampering for a grip.

CONSTANTINE roars and tosses away the table with surprising power.

In the corner GETHIN screams and covers his face.

CONSTANTINE (ROARING) He is mine! Mine! Never, never will he be yours, do you hear me? Never!

REMUS I'm... Have no...

CONSTANTINE Take your hordes! Take them. You see me stopping you? But he is mine, do you hear me. To do as I will!

REMUS is on all fours, a knife drawn ahead of him.

REMUS Cut you!

CONSTANTINE Do it then. Do it!

He bears his chest, egging the man on. In the corner GETHIN giggles.

The wind howls. A window breaks. The storm rages outside. Snow pours in through the hole. Both men turn to protect themselves from the driving snow and wind.

In the corner GETHIN screams.

The old man pulls his shirt around him again to protect from the cold.

REMUS rises, the knife still in front of him. He has to scream through the wind to make himself heard.

REMUS   She would not have liked this! She would not have you! He is hers! Do you hear me? Not mine! Not yours! Hers.

The knife in front of him still, he exits.

The door stays open. Snow is drifting in now, pouring into the room like water as we fade to black.

END OF ACT 3.

GREAT

ACT 4

SCENE 1

The past. The room as it was. Snow pulled through the broken window is piled over everything, but the storm is gone and the room is bathed in the summer tones of the past.

AMERICA, heavily pregnant. She stands at the table, feeling the baby inside her kick. She is singing a lullaby.

AMERICA Song birds, to parchment / sorrow songs to pillow-cases / Someone's departed, you become the broken hearted / Faces crack, summers lack, songs turn to chore / This is what we're looking after… / Kindness, to closed hands / Oaks turn to fire starters / King's crowns all fall down / You become another martyr / Hunger comes, rabbits run, water turns to hue / This is what we're looking after, this is what is coming after… / Song birds, to parchment…

The old man enters, girding himself for war. The armour is old and worn, almost ridiculous.

AMERICA stops singing and watches him as he bends and retrieves a sword wrapped in oil cloth from underneath the bed.

Ignoring her he takes it to the table and begins carefully to unwrap it.

AMERICA	(CONT.) I don't like this.
CONSTANTINE	Nor I.
AMERICA	The baby is close. I feel him.

Silence.

AMERICA	(CONT.) It's not your fight.

CONSTANTINE	No.
AMERICA	Then stay.
CONSTANTINE	Don't bite me woman! If the Village falls...
AMERICA	We are not the Village.
CONSTANTINE	Married there.
AMERICA	How many times...
CONSTANTINE	Stop biting at me. (Pause) It's decided.
AMERICA	And the baby?
CONSTANTINE	You are more than capable.

Silence.

AMERICA. (FINALLY EXPLODING) You... You... Old man! You would rather war than arms around me? Hold your son?

CONSTANTINE   He is mine. He will understand.

AMERICA   With winter... With winter closing every day, this is what you would rather do? This is where you would rather be? You... Old man! Do you think it will make you young again? Is that it, old man? Blood on your hands will make you young again? And how will you scare them? With your beard? Your pot belly? Are these the tools of war now? Is this what it's come to? Do young men look down from their horses, see a shuffling old goat and piss themselves? Coming towards them with a pig sticker and think the end is near? Is that it? Do they shudder at the sight of decrepitude and dream of surrender?

CONSTANTINE   I'll be back before winter.

AMERICA   You'll be back on your bed. Laid out bloody before me while your enemies sate themselves on me.

GREAT

On our child! (HE IS READY TO GO) Others would not leave me. You think the men of the Village would leave such a prize?

CONSTANTINE   Good, then. If I'm gone.

AMERICA   There are those that would have me.

CONSTANTINE   There are those who'd have peace if it were offered them.

AMERICA   Leave now and he is not yours.

CONSTANTINE   (ROUNDING ON HER) Where would you have me stand, woman! With my tail between my legs? In irons at your feet? Son or no, that is my blood and he will understand if I come back on a bed or no.

AMERICA   Perhaps.

Silence.

CONSTANTINE.   Perhaps?

AMERICA   Fight your war then.

CONSTANTINE   Say it again.

AMERICA   It was nothing.

CONSTANTINE   What was nothing.

AMERICA   Go then. See if…

CONSTANTINE   Perhaps?

AMERICA   You've made your decision.

Silence.

CONSTANTINE   That bald faced bastard!

AMERICA   No!

CONSTANTINE   Him, or another?

AMERICA   Husband…

CONSTANTINE   I should gut you!

AMERICA   The child is yours! I feel it!

CONSTANTINE   Aye, but you thought you'd make sure! Is that it?

AMERICA   I was scared.

CONSTANTINE   Ten thousand men may fall at my feet but I'll count them none until his blood is on me!

AMERICA   Husband…

He flings his arm, hitting her around the face carelessly. She falls in a heap, silent, and looks at him. He turns and marches out the door.

AMERICA   (CONT.) Husband!

She starts to stand, and then staggers back clutching her stomach in pain.

AMERICA   (CONT.) Husband!

She puts her hand down between her legs and it comes up bloody. She goes to move to the doorway and a sharp pain sends her clutching to the floor. She screams.

AMERICA   (CONT.) No, no, no, no, no! Not now!

She starts to shift position and another shard of pain drives her to the floor.

She is going into labour. The blood is clear and visible on her dress and the floor. She is breathing fast. Her face and arms covered in sweat and blood. In between contractions she turns herself to a sitting position on the floor and spreads her legs.

Each new contraction is stronger than the last, the blood now pooling from between her legs.

AMERICA   (CONT.) Come… Come on, then… Come on! You little bastard. You little shit. Come on, then. Come…

GREAT

A contraction drives her back and she screams out again. Her hand reaching between her legs as she feels the baby crowning.

AMERICA (CONT., IN TEARS) Fuck you, then. Fuck… You little shit. You little shit! I'm gonna…

She pushes hard driving the baby out of her. She screams. It falls with a thud between her legs and lies there. She falls back. The blood begins to pool once more.

All is still.

Then the baby cries.

AMERICA is raised by it.

She pulls herself to the table, the baby dragged along by the cord. She reaches up, takes the knife and cuts the cord. She never once touches the child.

Struggling, she rises. The baby is screaming on the floor. Steadying herself and bleeding badly, she steps over her child to the doorway.

The wind is picking up and it gusts snow outside.

She pauses, steadying herself, then steps out.

AMERICA (CONT.) CONSTANTINE!

Exit AMERICA.

The wind picks up to the tune of the baby's cries, and snow gusts in the door covering the bloody trail AMERICA left upon exiting. The only sight in the room now is the baby lying, crying in a pool of snow and its mother's blood.

Day turns to night.

CONSTANTINE returns.

The baby has quietened. The storm abated.

He stands at the door, bloody but triumphant from the battle and looks at his child lying in a pool of blood.

Taking the cloak from his back he moves to the child and collects him in its folds.

FADE OUT.

END OF SCENE 1.

SCENE 2

CONSTANTINE is sitting alone at the table.

The storm is at its zenith now. Snow piles in every corner. The door shakes and rattles. Flakes swirl throughout the stage.

REMUS enters. Squeezing in through the doorway he pins it shut with his body before turning his attention to the old man who has not moved.

From beneath his heavy coat, REMUS removes a box.

The box, no bigger than A4 in size, is an ordinary looking wooden box, but this is the lightning box, holder of all power, and it is treated as such by the men.

From the doorway REMUS, hesitant to enter, watches the old man.

REMUS	Constantine.
CONSTANTINE	You have it.
REMUS	I do. Though what...
CONSTANTINE	Drink?
REMUS	I think you'll stab me, no.
CONSTANTINE	Just drink.

Pause.

GREAT

REMUS — Alright then.

He sits at the table and puts the box on the table. Both men look at it while CONSTANTINE pours a drink.

CONSTANTINE — That's it?

REMUS — It is.

They drink. They refill.

CONSTANTINE — I ... I don't remember being young. I was once but... Memory is the death of you. You know this? It eats and it eats. As a young man it is... It is a kernel... This tiny side of you. And then it grows. No stopping it. (Beat) You begin to think. When you get older, you begin to think... And all that's there is memory. Memory on memory. Crushing. (HE DRINKS AND REFILLS) This doesn't help. So... Fuck it. Memory wins! Give up on today. Give up on it. Let the here and now... Wallow. (Pause) It does what you say?

REMUS — It does.

CONSTANTINE — God, she loved me. If she'd have seen me, coming back like that.... Vigour.

REMUS — You were... Young again.

CONSTANTINE — Last gasps of an old man. (BEAT) But with this...

The door is blown open, forced virtually off its hinges by the blizzard, and snow swirls around the room. The men cover to protect themselves. CONSTANTINE rises to close the door but GETHIN enters, a dead and frozen bird in his hands and manages to close it as much as is humanly possible against the driving snow.

The snow settles before anyone speaks.

GETHIN — I thought he don't come here no more.

CONSTANTINE	Get your things.

GETHIN holds up the small bird as if it were a prize.

REMUS	The Village is leaving, boy. You're coming with us.

GETHIN looks at CONSTANTINE.

CONSTANTINE	Get your things.
GETHIN	No.
REMUS	Boy...
CONSTANTINE	It's done.

The storm increases. The walls rattle. The door hammers at its hinges. Snow pours in through the broken window.

GETHIN	No!
REMUS	Listen to me boy...

GETHIN is beside himself. He shakes and begins to make whining noises which increase in intensity.

CONSTANTINE	Boy...
REMUS	Your father and...
CONSTANTINE	Listen to me boy...

In a swift move GETHIN flings the frozen bird at REMUS. He is shaking wildly now, rocking from side to side, the noises increasing, doing battle with the storm.

REMUS ducks the bird, unsure what to be more frightened of, the boy or the storm that is threatening to break the house.

REMUS	God... Constantine....

With a roar GETHIN flings himself at the man. A small rotten blade flashes in his hand. REMUS catches the knife arm just before it skewers him, but can do nothing about the other flailing appendages that batter him as the boy screams over the wind.

GREAT

The sound of the two men's momentary battle is almost drowned out by the storm.

CONSTANTINE brings the butt of his knife down on the back of the boy's head and he crumples to the floor, unmoving.

The storm abates slightly.

REMUS rises.

CONSTANTINE   Take him and go.

REMUS seems to have come to his senses. He looks around the cabin as if seeing it for the first time.

REMUS   Constantine...

But the old man turns away, his attention on the box on the table.

CONSTANTINE   Bind him if you value your eyes.

REMUS thinks about saying something but refrains. He pulls the dead weight of the boy up and hoists him on his shoulders.

The old man ignores him, his attention solidly on the box.

The room is shaking now, the storm threatening to tear it apart. At the door REMUS pauses and looks back at the old man alone at the table, the box in front of him.

He calls out.

REMUS   It's just memory. Come with us!

It's not clear if the old man has heard him or not and he calls again.

REMUS   (CONT.) CONSTANTINE! Come with us!

But there is no reply. Bracing himself, REMUS opens the door and struggles through into the storm, the unconscious boy slung over his shoulder.

The storm picks up. The door blows in.

The other window breaks and snow swirls over the stage, pushing in through every crevice.

The old man never moves.

Caught in a snowstorm, drifts piling up around his ankles, the old man opens the lightning box. An electronic warm glow radiates from within, lighting the old man's face as he is forever lost in an eternal white-out.

He watches the light as we lose him in the snow storm. An old man, alone with his memories, dying from the cold.

CURTAIN.

THE END.

THOMAS ALEXANDER – PLAYS

THE CROSSROADS COUNTRY

THOMAS ALEXANDER

A PLAY IN THREE ACTS

GOD

BY
THOMAS ALEXANDER

A COURTROOM DRAMA

DIRECT LIGHT

COMMEMORATIVE 450TH BIRTHDAY EDITION
A PLAY ABOUT LOVE, THEATRE & PLAGIARISM

Writing William

By

~~William Shakespeare~~ Thomas Alexander

INCLUDES FOREWORD BY AUTHOR,
DELETED SCENES & ORIGINAL PLAYBILL

The Family

THOMAS ALEXANDER

GREAT

THOMAS

Japan, 1945 – A Family At War

When a wandering priest escaping a troubled past is taken in by a prominent family, a quiet city in northern Japan is forced to confront the dark shadows of war seeping into their lives in ways they could never have anticipated.

With its townsmen scattered throughout the farthest ends of a desperate empire in a final defence against the encroaching West, the idyllic northern city of Morioka, far removed from the harsh realities of the front, is largely left to itself.

THOMAS ALEXANDER

A Scattering of Orphans

But when a prominent doctor is conscripted and sent to Manila, his sister is left as head of the household and must deal with a young priest living at the bottom of their garden with a large collection of maps and strange knowledge of English.

As the cold hand of war approaches, each person must choose their own destiny and place in the new world.

THE OTHER SIDE

ALEXANDER

Commemorating the 70th Anniversary of the end of WW2! A trilogy spanning the length of the war from the viewpoint of an ordinary Japanese family.

Offering a unique perspective through the eyes of a rural Japanese family into the impact of history's bloodiest war to date, *A Scattering of Orphans* is one family's attempt to make sense of a changing world amidst the desolation of war, both home and abroad.

OF THE SUN

www.ingramcontent.com/pod-product-compliance
Lightning Source LLC
Chambersburg PA
CBHW050902160426
43194CB00011B/2259